Language: English

These materials are designed to assist you in learning about hope. They should not be used for medical advice, counseling, or other health-related services. iFred, The Shine Hope Company and Kathryn Goetzke do not endorse or provide any medical advice, diagnosis, or treatment. The information provided herein should not be used for the diagnosis or treatment of any medical condition and cannot be substituted for the advice of physicians, licensed professionals, or therapists who are familiar with your specific situation. Consult a licensed medical professional, or call 911, if you are in need of immediate assistance.

ISBN: 978-1-954531-16-1

We would like to thank the following people for their contribution to our programs:

This program would not be possible without the brilliant leadership, support, and commitment to hope by:
Myron L. Belfer MD, MPA, Harvard Catalyst
Myron is Professor of Psychiatry in the Department of Psychiatry, Children's Hospital Boston, Harvard Medical School, and Senior Associate in Psychiatry at the Children's Hospital of Boston. Dr. Belfer is a Champion for Hope.

Kathryn Goetzke MBA, Author, Creator
Contributors: Taylor Steed, Katharine Lee-Kramer, Veronica O'Brien
Sarah Mellen, Mic Fariscal, Anna Termulo Montances and **Naneth Samoya-Jumawid**

To our advisors, hope contributors, and experts:
Dr. Edward Barksdale, Dr. Frank Gard Jameson, Mayor Hillary Schieve, Kristy L. Stark M.A., Ed.M., BCBA, Karen Kirby PhD, MSc, BSc, C.Psychol, AfBPS, SFHEA, Ulster University, **Marie Dunne** and the Northern Ireland team that helped plant the seeds for this work.

Pioneers in early Hope Science including **Dr. Crystal Bryce, Dr. Dan Tomasulo, Dr. Chan Hellman, Dr. Matthew Gallagher, Dr. Jennifer Cheavens and the late Dr. Shane Lopez.**

Lumanai, Désiré, & Harriet, Advisors
Toby, Noemi, Leeyah, Reese, & Mackenzie, Teen Contributors

Thank you to the iFred Board of Directors:
Tom Dean, Susan Minamyer, Jim Link, Dr. John Grohol, Kathryn Goetzke, Mindy Magrane

The Hopeful Minds Advisory Board

Some of our early funders: Sutter Health, Anthem, The Gordon Family Giving Fund of the Parasol Tahoe Community Foundation, The Shine Hope Company, and The Mood Factory.

IN SPECIAL RECOGNITION
Susan Minamyer, whose unconditional love, support, encouragement, faith, and brilliance planted and watered the seeds necessary to create and grow this program. Kathryn's big brothers **Arnold and Fred, and Clara, Maura, Jack, Sophie, Charles, and Sarah,** who continue to strengthen, build, and inspire Kathryn's hope.

IN HONOR
In recognition of all in the world that struggled with hopelessness in some way, shape or form, and left us way too early, including a few close to our hearts. Thank you for teaching us so much about life, love, and hope. May we spread Hope far and wide in your name and honor:
Jon and Sally Goetzke, Tom Foorman, Dr. Stephen C. Gleason, Vicky Harrison, Eloise Land, Jesse Lewis, and Austin Weirich.

Hey, amazing teens!

How ARE you?! Ugh, what a question these days. If you are dealing with some things, first off, please know you are not alone. The world seems to be in a bit of an upheaval, and I totally get it if you're mad, sad, frustrated, afraid, rageful, and whatever else. Makes total sense. That's why I worked with some amazing teens to create a manual to help you navigate it all.

Back in the day, I wished for a roadmap like this because I felt like I had no control as a kid and didn't have the skills to navigate life. This Hopeguide won't fix everything, but it'll light your path a bit. The Shine Hope™ framework and Hope Matrix keep me moving, even when things get tough, and I believe it can do the same for you.

Hope is not easy. It's about bravery, strength, and determination. If we don't practice these skills, we might turn to harmful stuff for relief. But facing our struggles, and using those emotions as rocket fuel to find our purpose—that's where real power lies. As if you focus that energy in the right way, I know you can move mountains.

One thing I want you to get from this guide is that moments of hopelessness are 100% normal. They occur throughout the day. It is when they become persistent that it is a problem. So we learn to proactively manage those moments, big or small, in healthy ways.

Ultimately, you're in charge of your life. Hope is about harnessing your emotions, fueling the power of them, and creating change. It is about learning what you care about, and figuring out how to do something about it. It's about setting and achieving your goals.

May this book serve to guide you on your journey in life, with tools to create a vision for anything in your future, fueled by positive feelings and inspired actions. So you are prepared to build a future for yourself, others, and the world you want to see. Sending you so much love on your journey.

And no matter what...

Keep Shining Hope,

Kathryn

TABLE OF CONTENTS

Welcome to Hopeful Minds 6

Hopeful Minds Definition List 8

Group Guidelines 10

My Shine Hope Hero 12

Module 1: The Science of Hope 15

Module 2: The Science of Hopelessness 31

Module 3: The Five Keys to Shine Hope 45

Module 4: The First Key to Shine Hope: Stress Skills 66

Module 5: The Second Key to Shine Hope: Happiness Habits 86

Module 6: The Second Key to Shine Hope: Happiness Habits Part 2 101

Module 7: The Third Key to Shine Hope: Inspired Actions 110

Module 8: The Third Key to Shine Hope: Inspired Actions Part 2 128

Module 9: The Fourth Key to Shine Hope: Nourishing Networks 142

Module 10: The Fifth Key to Shine Hope: Eliminating Challenges 160

Module 11: Using Resources to Shine 175

Module 12: Creating a Vision for your Future to Shine Hope 188

Resources 208

Welcome to Hopeful Minds

Thank you for choosing hope. Hope is a skill each and every person needs to learn, as it impacts all areas of life. By choosing this curriculum, you are taking the first step towards learning critical skills that will have lasting, positive impacts on your future. You can also earn service hours for the completion of this program, so we encourage you to take advantage of that opportunity.

The Hopeful Minds for Teens curriculum was tested and approved by teens, and is intended to give high school students a deeper understanding of the core components of hope. It was developed using hope theory informed by researchers around the world.

During adolescence, a crucial life stage, numerous teenagers undergo stress, which, if unaddressed, may evolve into anxiety and depression. Studies have found that anxiety and depression can begin to appear at age seven and continue to evolve throughout middle school. That is why it's important we teach hope during youth to protect against anxiety and depression. Check out our "what to look for' guide

**RESOURCES FOR STRESS,
ANXIETY, AND DEPRESSION**

Higher hope is associated with higher grades, improved attention in class, reduced likelihood of anxiety and depression, less violence in school, less likelihood of risky behaviors and addiction, better sports performance, less loneliness, and better quality relationships. Studies have found that anxiety and depression can begin to appear by age 7, and will continue to develop through middle school and high school. You can see the latest science and research on hope at Hopeful Minds *www.hopefulminds.org*

As you continue through this curriculum, you will see that every lesson includes:

- **Lessons:** The lessons introduce the Science of Hope and the Five Keys to Shine Hope.

- **Group Discussions:** The group discussions foster collaborative learning and give you a platform for sharing unique perspectives as you work through your hope journey. Use the note page at the end of each module to write down information generated from the group discussions.

- **Activities:** Games, puzzles, coloring, and creative expressive activities are embedded to help diversify the learning experience.

- **Self Reflections:** The reflections are designed to help you reflect on your hope journey, track your progress, and reinforce the lessons you've learned. Reflection questions for both individual and group reflection are included.

- **Hope Hero Spotlights:** Hope Hero Spotlights share the inspiring hope stories of actors, athletes, politicians, and more.

- **Inspired Actions for Hope:** Each lesson ends with inspired actions for hope: hope skills you can practice to begin to implement hope skills in your life. The more you practice the lesson's inspired actions, the easier it will be to create, maintain, and grow hope both during and after this course.

These lessons can be completed individually, as a group, or in a classroom setting. We encourage creativity, flexibility, and adaptability; the most important thing is that we teach the "how to" of hope. Hope must not be limited by access to resources; we must innovate when it comes to hope for all.

Hopeful Minds Definition List

The most important terms we use in our hope curriculum, and that we hope you will start using, include:

HOPE: We define hope as a vision for something in the future, fueled by both positive feelings and inspired actions.

HOPELESSNESS: Hopelessness is both a feeling of despair and a sense of helplessness. It is emotional (a negative feeling) and motivational (an inability to act). We all experience moments of hopelessness and manage them with hope skills.

POSITIVE FEELINGS: Positive feelings are those feelings that help us to stay hopeful as we work towards our goals.

INSPIRED ACTIONS: Inspired actions are the deliberate steps you take to get in your upstairs brains and toward your goals in life.

UPSTAIRS BRAIN: This is where our thinking, imagining, problem-solving, and learning occur. This part of the brain is responsible for the development of sound decision-making and planning, control over emotions and body, and self-understanding and empathy. The upstairs brain is also where we access our positive feelings.

DOWNSTAIRS BRAIN: Also referred to as the reptilian brain, this part of the brain is responsible for basic functions such as breathing, blinking, heart rate, and fight, flight, freeze, or fawn mode. It is also responsible for the chemical stimulus associated with strong emotions, such as anger, sadness, and fear.

STRESS RESPONSE: Your stress response is when an external or internal trigger causes your brain to release stress hormones, such as cortisol, adrenaline, and norepinephrine, that force you into your fight, flight, freeze, or fawn mode. It generally lasts 90 seconds from time of the last trigger.

STRESS SKILLS: These are actions that help you navigate your stress response and work through your body's chemical response to external stimuli, to get manage your downstairs brain and get you back upstairs.

HAPPINESS HABITS: These are healthy, long-term habits that help you stay in your upstairs brain, where you access the problem-solving skills, collaboration, and passion, all critical for hope. When you take time for Happiness Habits, your brain releases happiness hormones, such as endorphins, dopamine, serotonin, and oxytocin.

NOURISHING NETWORKS: Your Nourishing Networks are the Hope Networks of the people in your life that provide you with support, help you stay on track, encourage you to succeed, and who you do the same for in return.

ELIMINATING CHALLENGES: Challenges to Hope are negative thinking patterns, like limiting beliefs, automatic negative thoughts, all-or-nothing thinking, negative bias, rumination, worry, focusing on uncontrollables, attaching to outcomes, and internalizing failure, that can keep us in hopelessness states. Eliminating challenges are the conscious act of using hope skills to overcome these challenges and get back to hope.

THE HOPE MATRIX: The Hope Matrix is the process that we use to get from hopelessness to hope. The Hope Matrix teaches us that to cultivate hope, we must move from despair to positive feelings, and from helplessness to inspired actions.

Shine Hope™: This is the mnemonic we use to remember our hope skills. Shine stands for: Stress Skills, Happiness Habits, Inspired Actions, Nourishing Networks, and Eliminating Challenges and is what we use to activate skills for hope.

As you engage with the materials, we kindly request that you share the images from your hope guide on social media. This will aid us in learning and motivating others on the art of hope. Please tag *@ifredorg* and *@theshinehopecompany*, and include the designated hashtags *#hope #hopefulminds #ShineHope*. If you are a younger user, please obtain parental permission before posting on social media. We appreciate your commitment to embracing hope not just for yourself, but for those you influence and educate. Together, we can improve our collective future; hope is key to creating all we want.

Group Guidelines

Welcome, group members! Throughout this Hopeguide, you will work as a group to complete activities and reflect on materials, so the process of moving through the lessons will be highly collaborative. Each of you will have the role of fostering a positive and productive environment for all of the group members. Your goal as a group member is to ensure effective communication, active engagement, and a smooth workflow throughout the group's activities. This guide provides you with key strategies and tips to facilitate the group's collaboration successfully.

Ice Breaker Activity:

Ice Breaker activities are a great way to begin connecting and building relationships among group members. Check out two ice breaker activity options below.

Two Truths and a Lie:

Each person takes turns sharing three statements about themselves. The catch is that two of these statements are true, while one is a lie. Your goal is to trick others into believing the lie while presenting the truths in a convincing way. Feel free to be creative, but remember to keep your statements appropriate and respectful. After everyone has shared their statements, we'll have a discussion and reveal the lies. Get ready to learn some interesting facts about each other and have a great time connecting!

Would you Rather:

Take turns coming up with "Would you rather" scenarios, where every group member has to choose between two options. Each person takes turns answering the question and explaining their choice. Group members are encouraged to share their reasoning behind their decisions, sparking discussion and providing insight into their preferences. For example, you might ask, "Would you rather have the ability to fly or be invisible?" or "Would you rather travel to the past or the future?" Enjoy exploring different scenarios, discovering each other's perspectives, and engaging in lively conversations. Remember to create a friendly and inclusive atmosphere, and let the fun begin!

Group Expectations:

When working with a group, it's important to ensure that everyone is on the same page. As a group, develop a set of group expectations that each member will be expected to uphold throughout the duration of the Hopeguide. Examples of group expectations are that everyone shows up on time or that everyone takes turn sharing their ideas.

External Support:

While progressing through the curriculum, you might encounter strong emotions or obstacles. To assist your preparation, collaborate within your group to pinpoint available resources within your school or community that can be utilized during challenging times. List them in the box below:

My Shine Hope Hero

Choose a hope hero from your life, someone you admire like a famous athlete, musician, coach, teacher, or anyone you look up to. Write down their name below.

My Hope Hero is:

As you progress through this hope guide, engage in research by either having conversations with the person directly or conducting online searches (with permission from your parents). Look for examples of how your chosen hope hero has applied the skills taught in the Shine Hope framework, which you'll learn more about in lesson one. Return to this worksheet after each lesson and keep adding information until you've crafted a complete Hope Story for your hope hero. This process will help you understand how they've utilized hope skills to conquer challenges in their journey.

What is your hope hero hopeful for?

What does your hope hero experience moments of hopelessness about?

Module 1:
The Science of Hope

Module 1: The Science of Hope

What do you think of when you hear the word HOPE?

The true meaning of hope is misinformed by the media, who often use hope as a synonym for a wish. Exhibit A and B below.

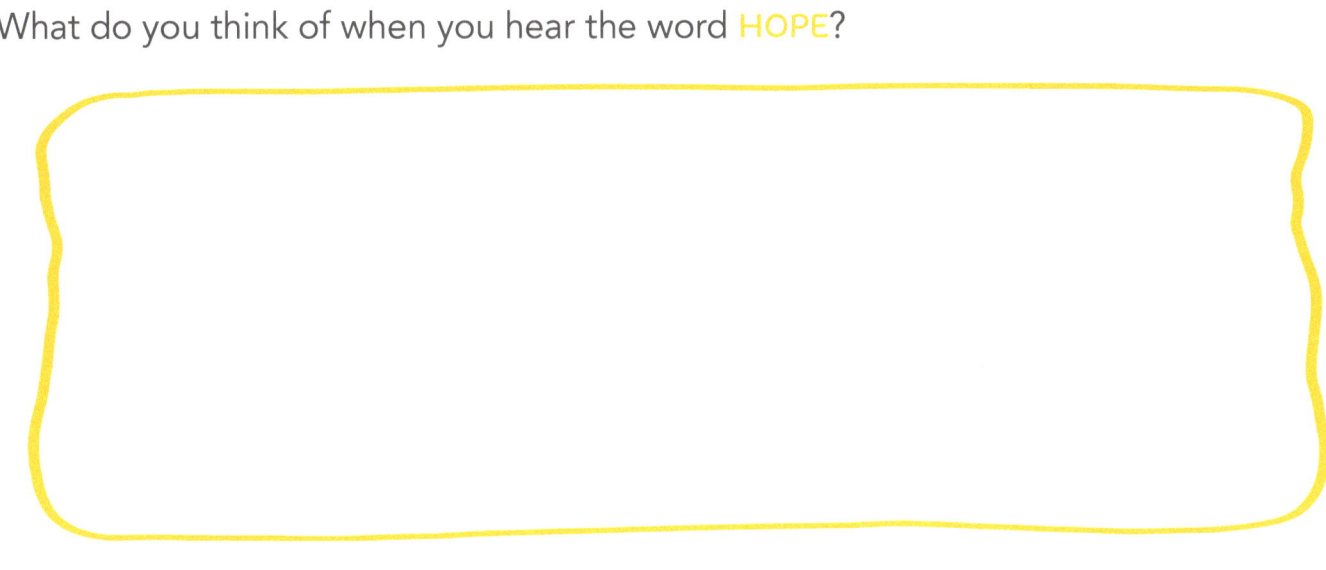

Dr. Stone Season 3: What We Hope to See in the Sequel

The third season of Dr. Stone will return shortly with even more exciting adventures. But what lies ahead for Senku and his companions?

Exhibit A

Anglers Hoping for Better Weather in February

Exhibit B

BUT, THIS ISN'T WHAT HOPE IS.

What we know:

HOPE ≠ WISH

HOPE is a vision for something in your future, fueled by both **POSITIVE FEELINGS** and **INSPIRED ACTIONS.**

When people exercise hope, they are not merely wishing for something to occur, they are cultivating positive emotions and taking action toward the goal they hope to achieve.

	MEASURABLE	TEACHABLE	TAKES INSPIRED ACTION	BASED ON LUCK	CONTROLLABLE
Wish	?	?	?	✔	?
Hope	✔	✔	✔	?	✔

HOW HOPEFUL ARE YOU?

Reflect upon your current level of hopefulness and shade in the option below that most accurately represents your degree of hope.

Not at all hopeful	A little hopeful	Pretty hopeful	Very hopeful!

SELF-REFLECTION

What are some reasons you want to increase hope within yourself?

Now let's see what science says.

Before you work through this Hopeguide, take the Hope measure now to see how your Hope score changes from the beginning of the Hopeguide to the end.

Use the link provided or scan the QR code (Page 196) to take the Snyder Hope Scale Assessment:

www.theshinehopecompany.com/measure-your-hope

My current Snyder Hope Scale Score:

How do you feel about your score?

How did your hope compare to how hopeful you thought you were?

How does it feel to know you have the power to change your hope score?

In this hopeguide, you will be taught the hope skills that you can use to create, maintain, and grow hope. No matter what hope score you received above, the goal of this course is to learn the "how-to" of hope both for yourself and others. This guide is not only a model for your own life; it is a framework you can use to share the power of hope with others.

WHY IS HOPE A BIG DEAL?

 People with higher hope set better goals for themselves and take the steps to meet those goals.

Researchers have also found a lot of neat positive outcomes related to higher levels of hope, such as:

 Improved academic achievement, above intelligence, personality, or previous academic achievement.

 Reduced hopelessness

 Improved athletic outcomes, beyond the athlete's training history, self-esteem, confidence, and mood

 Improved sleep

 Decreased recovery time following injuries

 Reduced risk of developing anxiety and depression

 Increased soccer-related reaction time.

 Reduced risk of sports-related injuries

 ## GROUP DISCUSSION

☀ *Is hope important in your life? How so?*

☀ *How does it feel to know you can improve your hope score?*

☀ *How does it feel to know that by understanding this program, you can help others improve their hope score?*

ALL ABOUT HOPE

40%

Percentage of teens in the US report persistent hopelessness since the start of COVID; Hope skills are known to help teens build relationships and fight loneliness.

One-third of teens have a mental health condition. Hope is a recognized protective factor for anxiety and depression, and it can reduce their symptoms.

Higher hope is believed to be the key to addressing climate change and the environmental crises.

More Hope leads to...

GPA INCREASE*
Above above intelligence, personality, and previous academic achievement

32%

MORE PRODUCTIVITY*
Above intelligence, optimism, and self-efficacy

14%

GOALS MET*
in a two-week period by people with average hope levels.

30%

Researchers have also found that higher hope lowers the risk of...

- Hopelessness
- Violence
- Addiction
- Suicide

- Chronic illnesses
- Early Death
- Sleep Difficulties
- Incarceration

- Dropping Out
- Stress
- Injuries
- and more...

*Curious to learn more about Hope research?
Check out our growing database at the Resources Page.

WHY WE MEASURE AND TEACH HOPE?

Hope is a measurable, teachable, and learnable skill. By measuring your hope, you are able to track your hope journey, monitor your progress, and reflect on how hopeful you are in the current moment. Hope is not fixed; when you practice hope skills, you can improve your hope score.

Our guide aims to teach you to increase your overall hope, which is enduring and persists across all situations regardless of the difficulty. Overall hope can help you have the skills to navigate all challenges you face in your life.

As you work through this Hopeguide, you will learn the skills needed to increase your hope. We use the mnemonic: **"Shine"** to teach the 'How' to hope. As long as you can remember to "Shine," you will always have hope:

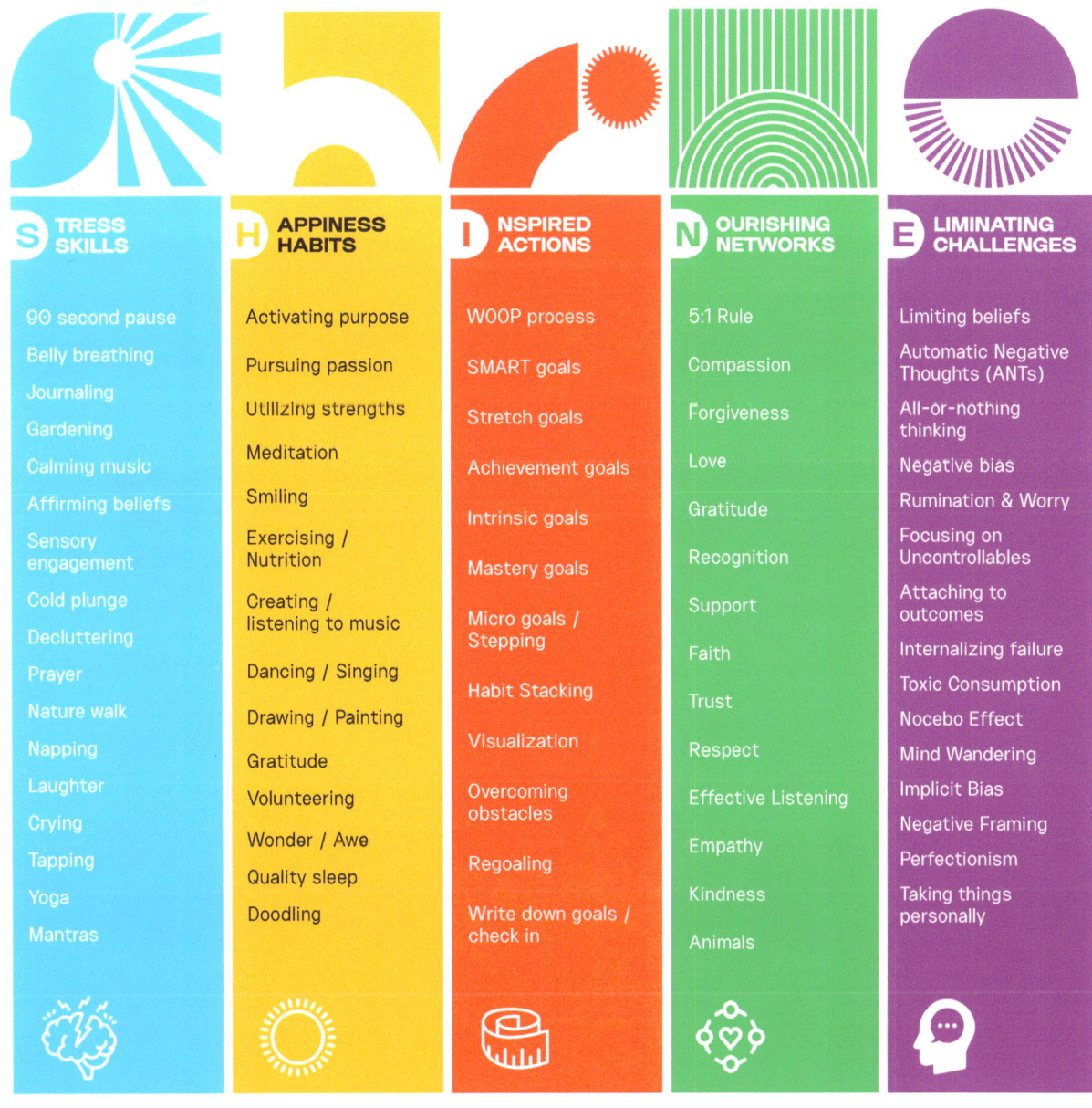

STRESS SKILLS	**H**APPINESS HABITS	**I**NSPIRED ACTIONS	**N**OURISHING NETWORKS	**E**LIMINATING CHALLENGES
90 second pause	Activating purpose	WOOP process	5:1 Rule	Limiting beliefs
Belly breathing	Pursuing passion	SMART goals	Compassion	Automatic Negative Thoughts (ANTs)
Journaling	Utilizing strengths	Stretch goals	Forgiveness	All-or-nothing thinking
Gardening	Meditation	Achievement goals	Love	Negative bias
Calming music	Smiling	Intrinsic goals	Gratitude	Rumination & Worry
Affirming beliefs	Exercising / Nutrition	Mastery goals	Recognition	Focusing on Uncontrollables
Sensory engagement	Creating / listening to music	Micro goals / Stepping	Support	Attaching to outcomes
Cold plunge	Dancing / Singing	Habit Stacking	Faith	Internalizing failure
Decluttering	Drawing / Painting	Visualization	Trust	Toxic Consumption
Prayer	Gratitude	Overcoming obstacles	Respect	Nocebo Effect
Nature walk	Volunteering	Regoaling	Effective Listening	Mind Wandering
Napping	Wonder / Awe	Write down goals / check in	Empathy	Implicit Bias
Laughter	Quality sleep		Kindness	Negative Framing
Crying	Doodling		Animals	Perfectionism
Tapping				Taking things personally
Yoga				
Mantras				

THE HOPE MATRIX

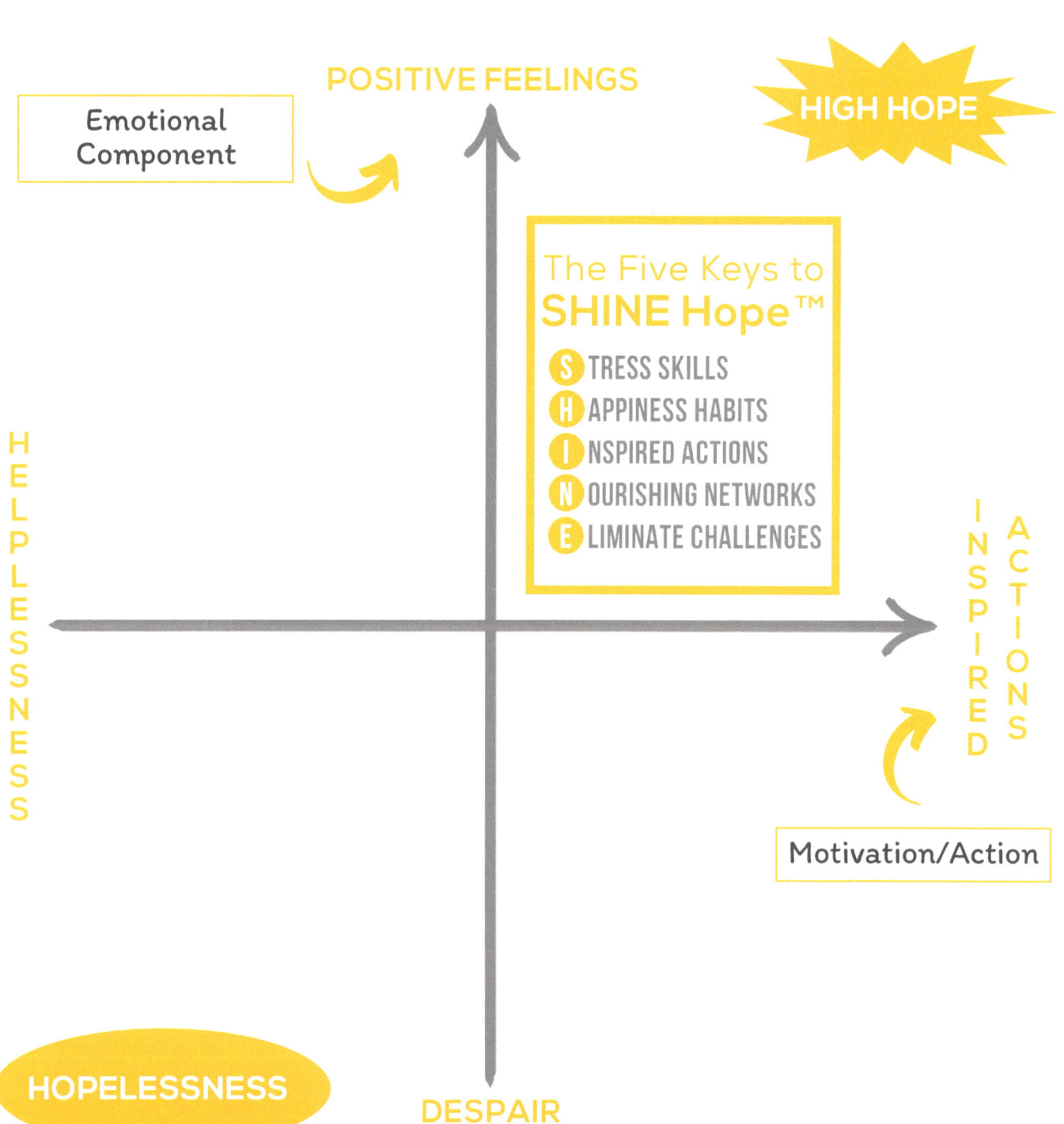

POSITIVE FEELINGS

HIGH HOPE

Emotional Component

The Five Keys to SHINE Hope™

S TRESS SKILLS
H APPINESS HABITS
I NSPIRED ACTIONS
N OURISHING NETWORKS
E LIMINATE CHALLENGES

HELPLESSNESS

INSPIRED ACTIONS

Motivation/Action

HOPELESSNESS

DESPAIR

IDENTIFYING YOUR STRENGTHS

Recognizing your strengths is essential for creating and maintaining hope. Focusing on your strengths can help you manage your stress response, cultivate Happiness Habits, and focus on the future. As you continue through this workbook, you will repeatedly be asked to reflect on your strengths.

Take a moment to learn more about your strengths by taking the free VIA Character Strengths Survey here or scan the QR code at Page 196:

www.theshinehopecompany.pro.viasurvey.org

Write down the top five strengths identified in your results:

1

2

3

4

5

Which of these strengths do you think is most tied to your ability to maintain hope?

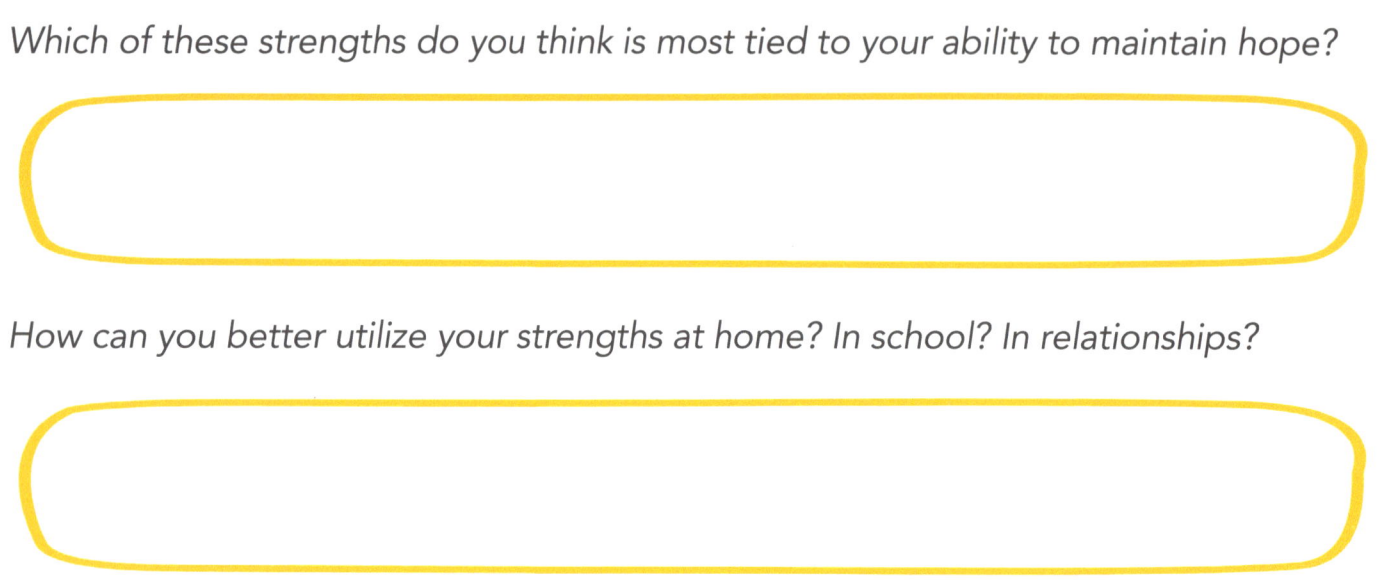

How can you better utilize your strengths at home? In school? In relationships?

GROUP ACTIVITY

☀ *Have the group guess each member's number one strength.*

☀ *Have each group member give an example of how they show their strength in their day-to-day life.*

THE SYMBOL FOR HOPE: SUNFLOWERS

We were very deliberate in our choosing of the sunflowers. It all began from a study by the Emotional Impact of Flowers Study conducted by Jeannette M. Haviland-Jones, Ph.D., Professor of Psychology, Project Director, Human Development Lab at Rutgers. According to her research, regardless of age, flowers have an immediate impact on happiness. Recent studies have suggested flowers help reduce stress, and often increase serotonin and dopamine. As we further researched, we found:

- The symbolism of the sunflower holds a deep meaning. A sunflower seed begins its journey in darkness, mirroring our most hopeless states. It represents our potential for growth and improvement amid despair. Just as a seed cannot flourish alone, we, too, rely on our Hope Network to nurture our hope.
- The growth of a sunflower echoes our journey toward hope. It stretches roots deep into the ground, similar to our efforts to break free from despair using Stress Skills—meditation, deep breathing, and mindful pauses.

- As the sunflower emerges into the sunlight, it unfurls leaves to gather sunshine, needing water, nourishment, and care to flourish. Similarly, we cultivate positive feelings through Happiness Habits—long-term, healthy practices fostering more and more hope.
- Obstacles pepper the sunflower's path: rocky soil and inadequate resources. Likewise, we face challenges. However, equipped with Stress Skills, Happiness Habits, Inspired Actions, Nourishing Networks, and skills to Eliminate Challenges, we approach and conquer these hurdles.
- The sunflower also provides sustenance and joy just like how we share hope with those around us, becoming beacons of optimism and joy.
- Our choice of the sunflower and its vibrant yellow hue symbolizes our commitment to shine a positive light on hope, eradicating mental health stigma through proactive measures in prevention, research, and education. Yellow is the color of happiness and hope.
- Gardening is also very healthy for mood, so we encourage community gardens. Eating sunflower seeds can be healthy for the brain, as they are rich in vital nutrients. It is also one of the only flowers that can be planted anywhere in the world, and we believe the 'how' to hope must be planted everywhere as well.
- It is also a method for nonprofits to raise funds for hope. You can sell the seeds, have gardens sponsored, sell products in retail, or create art for auctions. The ideas are endless!

So, in this endeavor, the sunflower becomes the embodiment of hope, illuminating pathways toward a brighter future for individuals.

PLANT SUNFLOWER GARDENS TO SHINE HOPE

Gardening is a great time to practice the Shine Hope Framework, as we have a lot of challenges while planting a garden and we can go from hope to hopelessness pretty quickly. Yet that is a normal part of life, so gardening is an easy place to start practicing these skills.

Say you find some tough ground you need to dig into to plant, you may get frustrated and give up. It is a good time to practice a **Stress Skill** like a 90-second pause or deep breathing, to calm down your stress response. Then try again! You may also notice when others get frustrated and teach them how to use this skill to navigate from their downstairs brain back upstairs.

Eating the sunflower seeds (if ok with your doctor) might be a good way for you to practice your **Happiness Habits.** Sunflower seeds are nutritious, high in choline and selenium, great for brain function and memory. You might also get some exercise planting gardens, and spend time in nature, two other Happiness Habits and great ways to release endorphins.

Planting gardens remind us to take **Inspired Actions** by setting specific goals for the garden. If we want a garden, we need to set a SMART goal about how many flowers, when and where we want the garden, and how we are going to grow the flowers. It is best if we write down the plan, chunk it down into actionable steps, think about obstacles and multiple ways we might overcome them, and check in with someone regularly to ensure progress.

We can cultivate our **Nourishing Networks** by planting gardens with others. That way, if we have challenges while planting, we can face them together and be more creative about overcoming them. And if we don't live by the person we want to plant with, we can both decide to plant and check in regularly on the garden. It is also super fun to plan community gardens, or even fields of sunflowers, and all join together in learning and practicing skills to Shine Hope.

And finally, time to get serious about **Eliminating Challenges**. For example, if our sunflowers die and we fail for a season of planting, it is easy for us to think of ourselves as failures. Yet we aren't failures, our process failed. So deconstruct the process. Did we under or over water? Did we plant at the wrong time of year? Was something wrong with the soil? Did we overwater? It is time to investigate, and instead of ruminating about the sunflowers start figuring out what we can do better to try again next year.

Planting sunflowers is a way to spread the message of hope, as if you put up a Gardens of Hope sign with the website, people can then find the curriculum to learn more about the programs for 'how' to hope. Our program is available around the world, and gardens are a great way to share the message that Hope is Teachable.

HOPE HERO SPOTLIGHT

JOHN KRASINSKI

Several years ago, actor John Krasinski was watching the news when he realized that the news channels only focused on sad stories, even when there were many good things going on in the world. He wished the news would report more happy stories, but he couldn't do anything about it.

When the corona virus pandemic began, he watched as the news got even sadder. He realized it was time to stop wishing the news would be happier and start hoping for it. What's the difference? John used positive feelings and inspired actions to create a positive news channel.

Specifically, John followed the Shine Hope Framework and created Some Good News, which is a news broadcast (shot from John's home office) that focuses on happy things happening worldwide. John's Stress Skills and Happiness Habits involved sharing positive stories and he took Inspired Actions to spread his Happiness Habit of feel-good stories. He threw virtual parties for students who graduated, and nurses and doctors who were working hard to fight COVID-19. John shared stories about recoveries, let people video chat with their favorite celebrities and shared the happy videos people sent him.

John didn't just wish the news would change; he hoped for happier news stories, and he used his positive feelings and inspired actions to make it happen. *

This story was created from publicly available information. It does not suggest endorsement of Hopeful Minds, or any affiliation by known celebrity to our program. All information is for illustrative purposes for youth, to demonstrate skills used to create, maintain, and grow hope.

☀ *What is one piece of information you found most helpful in this lesson?*

☀ *How will you incorporate the information you learned in this lesson to your life this week?*

☀ *John Krasinski used the Shine Hope Framework to create Some Good News. What do you hope to accomplish using the Shine Hope framework?*

☀ *What are barriers that might keep you from working through the Hopeguide? How can you address those barriers?*

Go back to the very first worksheet on page 11, where you identified your hope hero. Fill in what you believe your hope hero is hopeful for.

WEEKLY HOPE ACTIVATION

Inspired Actions for Hope are the things you can do to reinforce these lessons and begin to bring hope skills into your daily life. Choose at least one of the actions below to complete before moving to the next lesson.

☀ Collect hope quotes, and put them on the wall.

☀ Create a video montage of what your group Hopes for.

☀ Exchange workbooks and write each other Hope notes in the extra pages at the back of this Hopeguide.

☀ Paint a sunflower mural for hope *(Page 196)*

☀ Plant a sunflower garden *(Page 196)*

☀ Check out our Hopeful Cities program *(Page 196)*

NOTES

Post your completed activities on social media using the following hashtags to help us teach the lessons. Make sure to tag us **@ifredorg** and **@theshinehopecompany.**

#HopefulMindsTeens #Hope #ShineHope #HopeScience #Sunflower #HopeMatrix #MeasureHope #HopeGuide #TeenMentalHealth #Prevention

Module 2:
The Science of Hopelessness

Module 2: The Science of Hopelessness

THE HOPE MATRIX CONNECTION

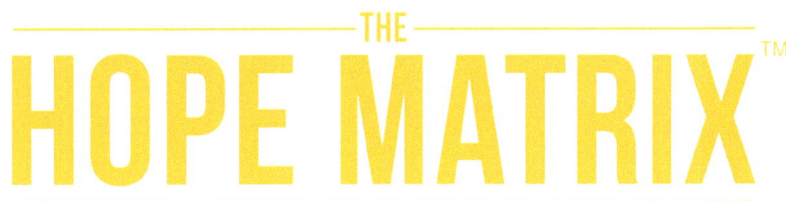

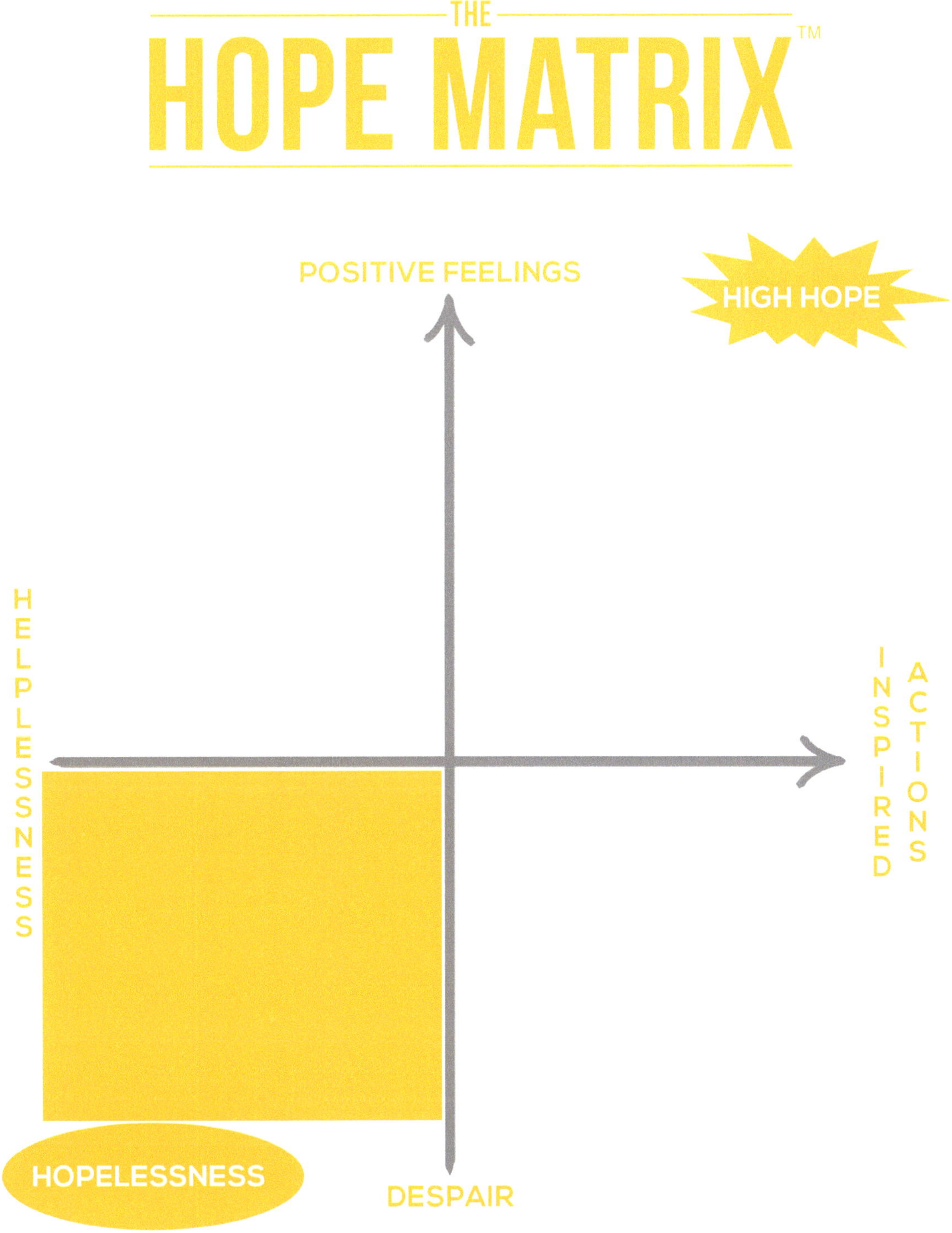
THE
HOPE MATRIX™
POSITIVE FEELINGS
HIGH HOPE
HELPLESSNESS
INSPIRED ACTIONS
HOPELESSNESS
DESPAIR

WHAT IS HOPELESSNESS?

Before we dive into hope and its skills, we must first look at what happens in the absence of hope: hopelessness. Many people talk about hopelessness, but do you really know what it is? When people say they are hopeless, what does that even mean? Most people think of hopelessness as a feeling of "despair." Yet that isn't the full story.

 **HOPELESSNESS** is characterized by **EMOTIONAL DESPAIR** *(sadness, anger, fear)* and **MOTIVATIONAL HELPLESSNESS** *(a sense of powerlessness)*

That is why to address hopelessness, you need to talk about both feelings and actions.

Directions: Below, color in the words using colors you associate with the word hopelessness. In the circle, draw an emoji that you think is associated with hopelessness.

HOPELESSNESS
Emotional Despair and Motivational Helplessness

HOPELESSNESS IS NORMAL

Everyone, without exception, experiences moments of hopelessness. It's something that all of us go through even daily. It's important to understand this because it reminds us that we're all experiencing it, **it's what we do with the moments of hopelessness that matters.**

Various things can trigger hopelessness. Sometimes it is caused by significant life events like the loss of a loved one. Other times, hopelessness is caused by smaller challenges we face in our daily lives, such as receiving a low grade on a test, having a fallout with a friend, or not making a team. Even things like getting stuck in traffic, getting the flu, or being late can trigger a moment of hopelessness.

External factors can also contribute to persistent feelings of hopelessness. This includes things like discrimination, oppression, the impact of a global pandemic, or concerns about global warming. These larger issues can make us feel like our efforts are ineffective or that the world is too overwhelming to handle.

Additionally, internal factors can play a role in experiencing hopelessness. Negative emotions, physical pain, or being faced with difficult decisions can all contribute to a sense of hopelessness. It's important to recognize that these internal struggles can affect our outlook on life.

Remember, it's completely normal to feel hopeless at times, and it doesn't mean there's something wrong with you. It's part of being human.

 ## GROUP DISCUSSION

☀ *What are other common events that may trigger moments of hopelessness in your lives?*

☀ *What do you notice about your emotions and how your body feels when you have moments of despair?*

☀ *What do you notice about your experience of helplessness and what are your thoughts about that helplessness?*

☀ *What do you notice about the combination of despair and helplessness (i.e., the two ingredients of hopelessness)?*

Given that moments of hopelessness are so common, our goal is to help you develop tools and strategies to move past the moments and find your way back to hope.

We all have these moments of hopelessness and they look different for everyone. Draw an emoticon that represents how you feel in these situations:

MOMENTS OF HOPELESSNESS

Not making a sports team

Being late for school

A friend says something mean

MORE SIGNIFICANT EXPERIENCES OF HOPELESSNESS

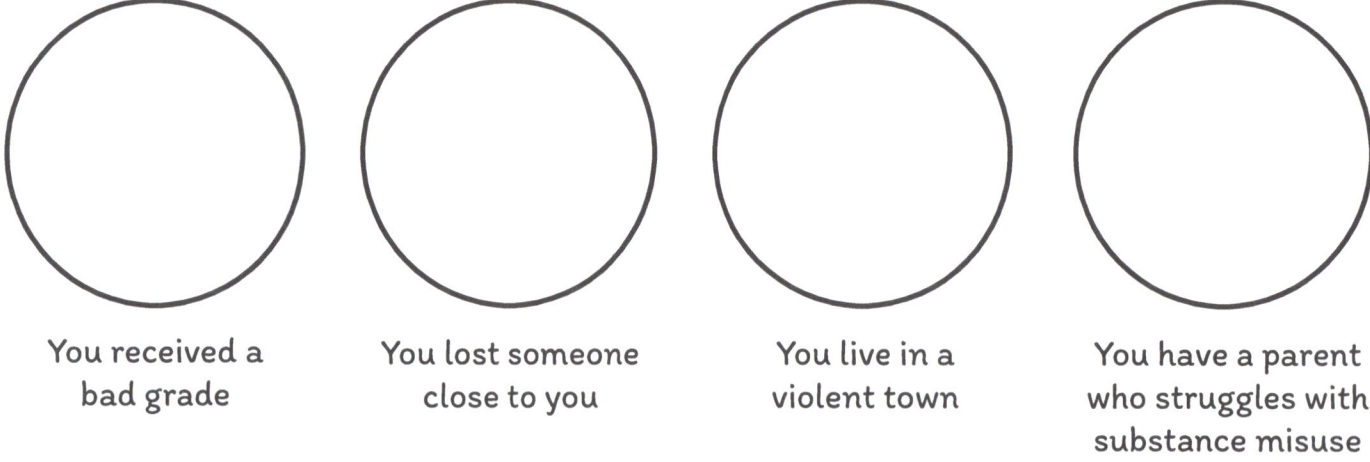

You received a bad grade

You lost someone close to you

You live in a violent town

You have a parent who struggles with substance misuse

It's how we manage hopelessness that matters. If we are not proactive about hopelessness, it can lead to various disorders. Persistent hopelessness is related to anxiety, depression, or suicidal ideation, so it's really important we work to manage the hopelessness that everyone experiences. And we need to understand that it is okay to seek support to manage hopelessness, especially if we are going through a more significant life experience.

Some groups are also more susceptible to persistent hopelessness, making it even more important to ensure every single person has the skills to move from hopelessness to hope.

3 out of 5 teen girls in the United States
report persistent hopelessness

Discrimination and Oppression
within minority groups leads to persistent hopelessness

2 out of 5 teens in the USA
report persistent hopelessness

☀ *What strategies have you used in the past to successfully manage moments of hopelessness (i.e., despair and helplessness)?*

☀ *What resources are available when you are struggling to manage moments of hopelessness?*

☀ *Sometimes, things that lead to moments of hopelessness can't be changed, like a poor test grade, what action can you take in those situations to help manage the hopelessness?*

*See the end of this lesson for additional resources.

LIMITING BELIEFS vs AFFIRMING BELIEFS

Sometimes, when we are faced with moments of hopelessness, we experience limiting beliefs. Limiting beliefs are those thoughts that make you doubt yourself or think you can't do something. For example, "I'm not smart enough to pass this test." They hold you back, make you feel stuck, and can prolong the moment of hopelessness.

On the other hand, affirming beliefs are the positive thoughts that boost your confidence and tell you that you're capable of achieving your goals. For example, "This material is really hard, but I know I'm capable of studying and learning the material to pass the test."

When you fill your mind with limiting beliefs, it's like putting up roadblocks on the path to hope. They make you feel like there's no way things can get better. But when you recognize the limiting beliefs, you can change them to affirming beliefs, allowing you to open the door to hope.

GROUP ACTIVITY

Practice changing the following Limiting Beliefs to Affirming Beliefs.

Education doesn't matter; I won't get anywhere anyway

My family has always been poor, so I'll never be able to afford college.

I'm not interesting enough for people to want to be friends with me

I messed up a presentation, so everyone probably thinks I'm not smart.

GROUP DISCUSSION

☀ *What are negative things people have told you about yourself, and how has that lead to a Limiting Belief?*

☀ *What are some Limiting Beliefs you've had? How did those Limiting Beliefs shape your mood?*

☀ *How were you able to move past the Limiting Belief?*

☀ *What are positive things you want to believe about yourself, and how does it lead to Affirming Beliefs?*

☀ *List out Affirming Beliefs next to the Limiting Beliefs you wrote above, and commit to rehearsing the Affirming Beliefs until you believe them.*

HOPELESSNESS AND HORMONES

Moments of hopelessness are normal, and there's a biological reason why teens experience more of these moments.

There is a lot of development that goes on during the teenage years. One of the biggest changes your body goes through is puberty.

Around the time of puberty, your body starts to produce an influx of the hormones estrogen or testosterone which can have a lot of power over your emotions and behaviors. The fluctuations in these hormones can lead to increased mood shifts, impulsiveness, and even aggression and violence.

One of the reasons you may experience more negatively charged emotions because your teenage years are a time when you are under an immense amount of stress as you begin to form your identity, manage academic workloads, and navigate relationships with family and peers.

As you face this time in life with increased stressors and hormone changes, it becomes more important now than ever to start recognizing moments of hopelessness so you can manage the moments and work to prevent chronic negatively charged emotions and potentially risky behaviors. Maintaining hope starts with becoming more aware of the moment of hopelessness.

In the following vignettes, discuss the signs of hopelessness. What are the emotions? And where is the powerlessness?

Vignette #1
Taylor is a 9th grade student who just transferred to a new high school. At her old school, she had a lot of friends and was heavily involved in extracurricular activities (i.e., theater, softball, band). Taylor wanted to continue with her extra curricular activities to build relationships but her new school didn't offer these activities. Taylor began to feel increasingly sad as she struggled to find ways to connect with her peers. Months passed by and Taylor struggled to find ways to make meaningful relationships at school, she felt isolated and disconnected from her peers. Taylor's goal of making friendships faded and she no longer felt the energy to try. She felt trapped in a cycle of disappointment and soon her motivation for school was affected as she no longer saw the point in trying at school.

Vignette #2
Jacob sat alone at his desk, his head resting on his hand as he stared blankly at an unfinished assignment. Jacob once had a bright spark in his eyes that has since dulled and been replaced with weariness. The weight of his academic struggles is heavy on his shoulders, making each breath feel heavier than the last. As Jacob moves in the lively hallway between classes, he feels invisible and lost, as if others do not notice his existence.

Each day that passes, Jacob feels more disappointment and frustration with his school performance. Jacob aimed to attend a university, and this goal now feels unmanageable. With each failed test, Jacob's confidence crumbles, and he feels lost as to what to do next.

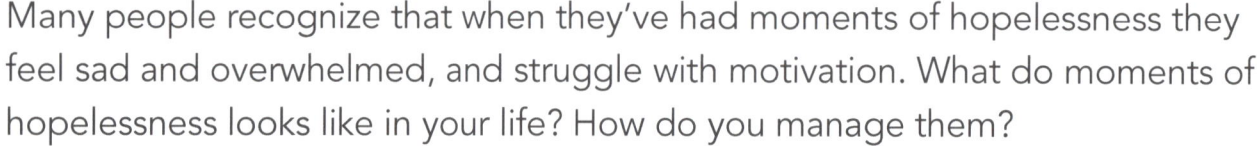

Many people recognize that when they've had moments of hopelessness they feel sad and overwhelmed, and struggle with motivation. What do moments of hopelessness looks like in your life? How do you manage them?

When faced with moments of hopelessness, what does your motivation look like? How do you manage feeling powerless? How did you manage these?

HOPE HERO SPOTLIGHT

DWAYNE "THE ROCK" JOHNSON

It is easy to look at successful celebrities and assume that they have it all figured out. However, no one is immune to the effects of helplessness and despair, the two ingredients of hopelessness. It is our ability to proactively manage hopelessness that allows us to continues to find hope and achieve our dreams. Just look at Dwayne "The Rock" Johnson.

Dwayne is a famous wrestler and actor. However, in his teen years, before he found success, his family struggled to make ends meet. In an attempt to support his family, he turned to crime to make money quickly. He was arrested several times, and descended into a pit of hopelessness. It would have been easy for Dwayne to remain trapped in his cycle of negative emotions and actions.

However, Dwayne instead managed his hopelessness and focused on training for his long term goals of playing football professionally then getting into wrestling. He realized that if he truly wanted to help his family, he needed to find ways to support them long term, and he couldn't do that from prison. Every time Dwayne faced an obstacle that made him feel hopeless, he used positive feelings and inspired actions to return to hope and keep moving forward.

Just like Dwayne, we do not have to be defined by our times of hopelessness. We can learn to manage our helplessness and despair, and maintain hope.*

*This story was created from publicly available information. It does not suggest endorsement of Hopeful Minds, or any affiliation by known celebrity to our program. All information is for illustrative purposes for youth, to demonstrate skills used to create, maintain, and grow hope.

LESSON TAKEAWAY (GROUP DISCUSSION):

☀ *What is one piece of information you found most helpful in this lesson?*

☀ *How will you incorporate the information you learned in this lesson to your life this week?*

☀ *Dwayne Johnson talks about how he managed hopelessness using sports. How will you manage moments of hopelessness?*

Go back to the very first worksheet on page 11, where you identified your hope hero. Fill in what you believe your hope hero has moments of hopelessness about.

WEEKLY HOPE ACTIVATION

Inspired Actions for Hope are the things you can do to reinforce these lessons and begin to bring hope skills into your daily life. Choose at least one of the actions below to complete before moving to the next lesson.

☀ Think about situations where you are most likely to feel hopelessness and write them down. Awareness of those triggers can help you fight hopelessness before it becomes persistent.

☀ Think about challenges or obstacles you may face while working through this Hopeguide. Plan how you will overcome those challenges or obstacles to continue your journey toward hope. Write this plan down and hang it on your wall or locker.

☀ Ask three people in your life about a moment of hopelessness. Everyone feels hopeless at some point in their life, and it's important to recognize how common it is. Ask them how they overcame hopelessness.

☀ Find out what resources are available in your school or community to support you during challenging times. Tell at least one other person about these resources.

NOTES

Post your completed activities on social media using the following hashtags to help us teach the lessons. Make sure to tag us **@ifredorg** and **@theshinehopecompany.**

#HopefulMindsTeens #Hope #ShineHope #ScienceofHope #Hopelessness #TeenMentalHealth #HopeIsTeachable

Module 3:
The Five Keys to Shine Hope

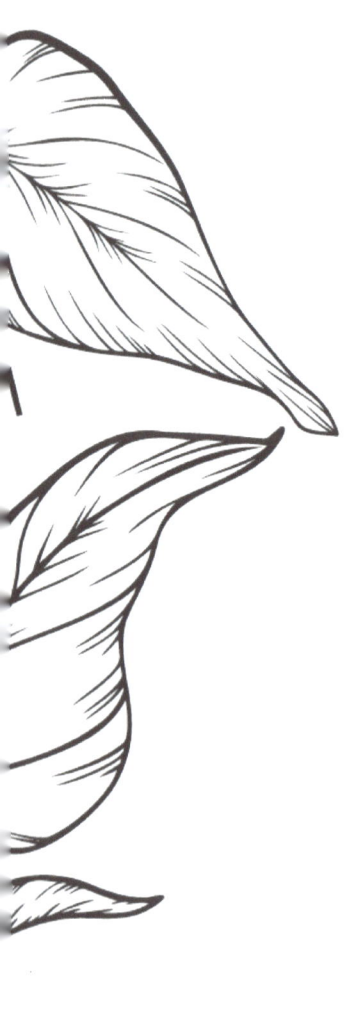

Module 3: The Five Keys to Shine Hope

Emotions are a big part of the Shine Hope framework. As we learned in module 1, hope is partly defined by positive feelings, and we can achieve positive feelings through each of the Five Keys to Shine, but first let's learn a bit more about emotions in general.

MAPPING ONTO THE HOPE MATRIX

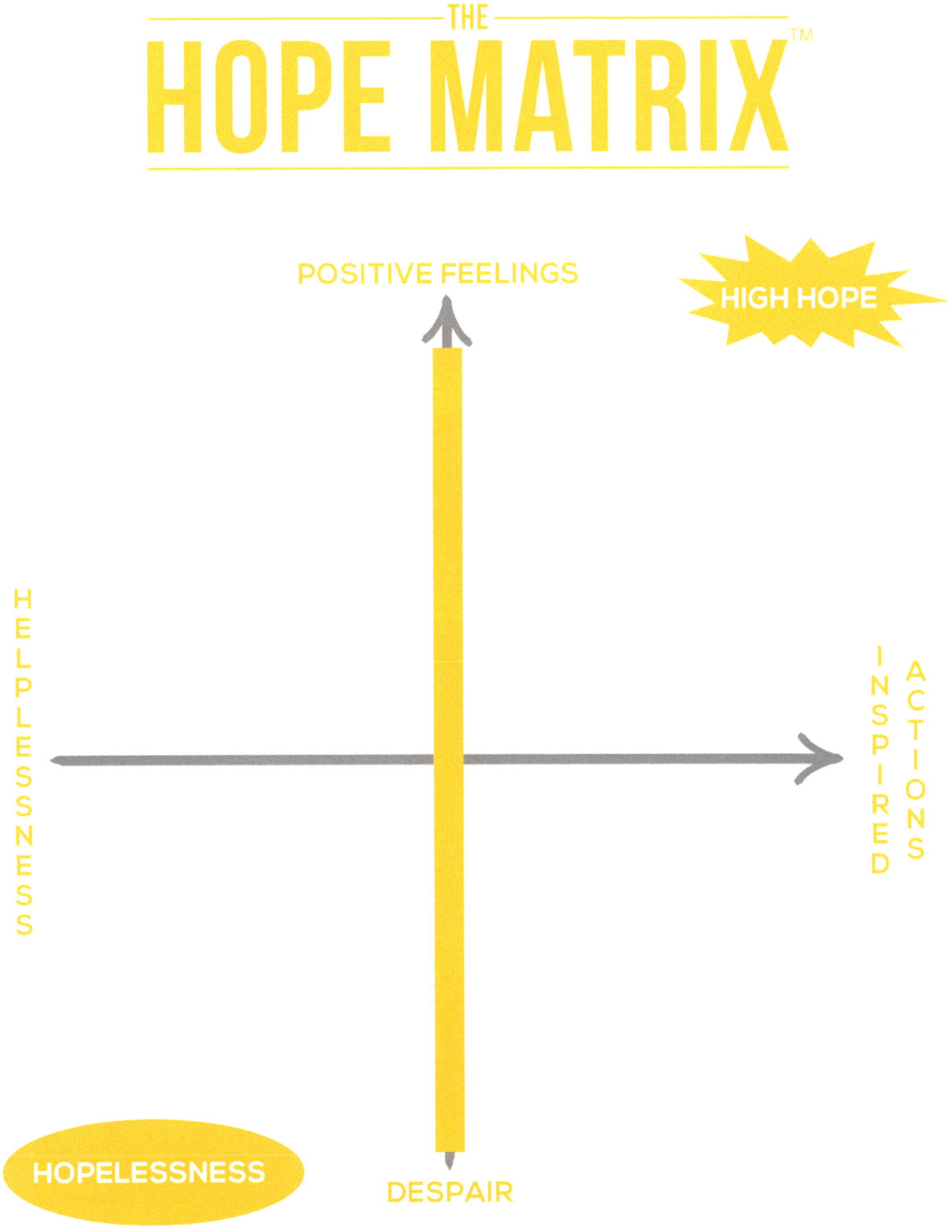

THE
HOPE MATRIX™

POSITIVE FEELINGS

HIGH HOPE

HELPLESSNESS

INSPIRED ACTIONS

HOPELESSNESS

DESPAIR

WHAT'S THE DEAL WITH EMOTIONS?

Emotions are a part of the human experience, We ALL experience emotions. Although we sometimes experience negatively charged emotions that are not so fun, like stress or sadness, emotions are a vital part of how our brain works.

We have primary emotions and secondary emotions. Think of primary emotions as the basic colors on an artist's palette that everyone can recognize and experience. They are like the building blocks of our emotional responses.

Secondary emotions, on the other hand, are a bit more complicated. They're like mixing colors together to create new shades and tones. Secondary emotions come from a mix of primary emotions and our thoughts, beliefs, and interpretations.

It's like when you feel a combination of sadness, fear, and anger when you're ashamed or guilty about something. These emotions can be influenced by our own experiences, cultural backgrounds, social norms, and personal beliefs. They're more personalized and can be a bit trickier to understand.

Directions:

1. The center of the sunflower lists our primary emotions. Color the positively charged emotions one color and the negatively charged emotions a second color.

2. The petals of the sunflower list our secondary emotions that came from the primary emotion. Spend time looking over them while coloring the petals.

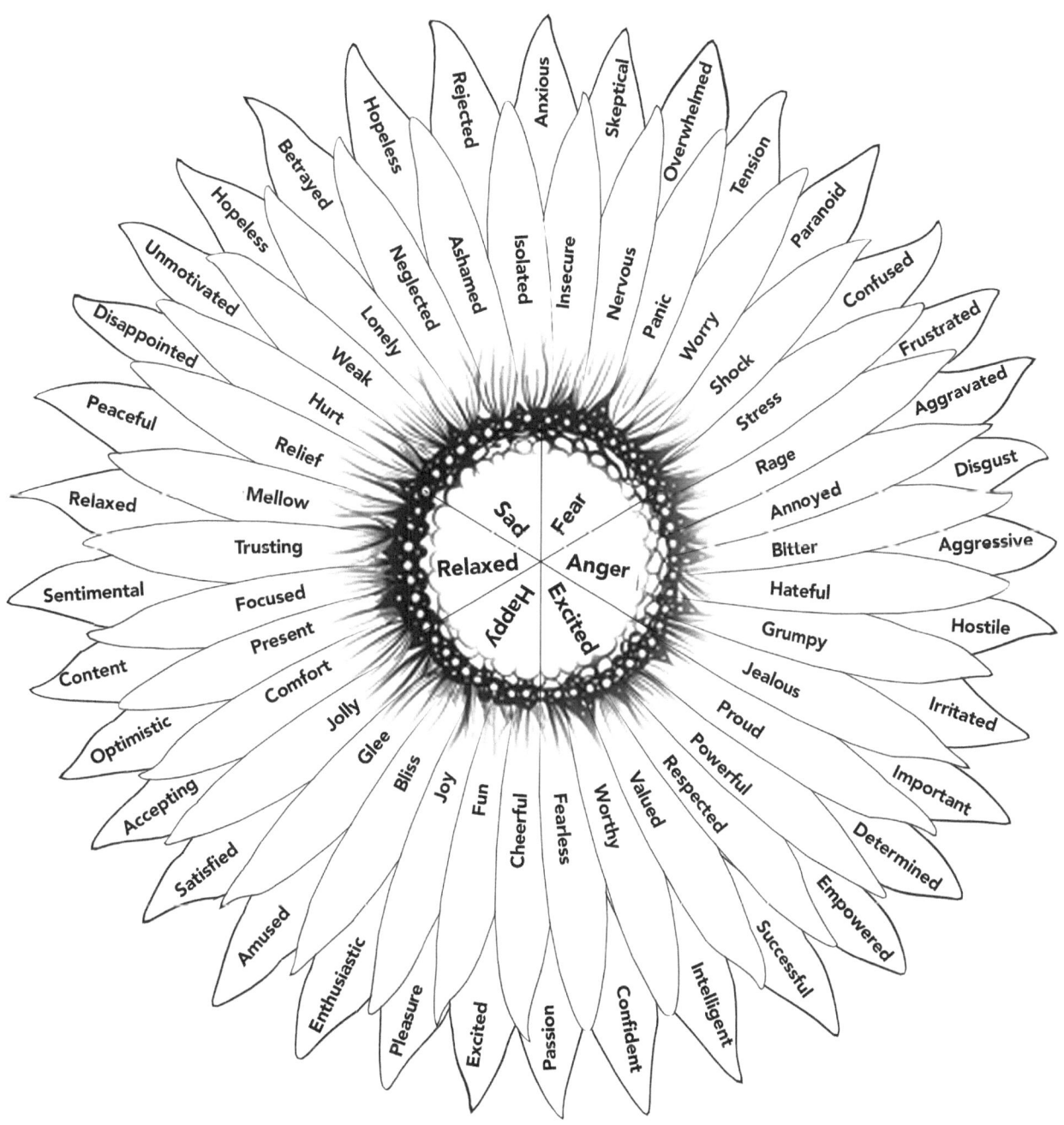

Remember, emotions are unique to each person, and how we experience and interpret them can be different from one another. So, while primary emotions are like the basic building blocks, secondary emotions add depth and complexity to our emotional experiences.

Emotions serve important purposes in our lives and are important in building hope skills. They provide valuable information about ourselves and the world around us, guiding our decision-making and motivating us to set goals and take action.

Emotions help us form connections with others, communicate our needs, and navigate relationships. They also act as a warning system, protecting our safety and well-being. Understanding and embracing our emotions can help us navigate the teenage years with greater self-awareness and resilience.

PURPOSE OF NEGATIVELY CHARGED

While negatively charged emotions often don't feel good,
they serve important purposes.

Anger

Helps protect us and set boundaries, while also motivating us to make positive changes and communicate our feelings.

Fear

Fear serves as a protective instinct, alerting us to potential dangers and helping us stay safe. It can motivate us to take necessary precautions and make informed decisions, enabling personal growth and resilience in the face of challenges.

Sadness

Allows us to acknowledge and process difficult emotions. It can help us heal, gain insights about ourselves, and seek support from others to navigate challenging situations.

GROUP DISCUSSION

☀ Can you recall a situation when you experienced a blend of emotions, like feeling both angry and sad or ashamed and guilty? How did those emotions interact with each other?

☀ Are there any secondary emotions that you find particularly challenging or complex? Why do you think that is?

☀ Share an example from your life when a primary emotion developed into a secondary emotion. How did it happen, and what impact did it have on you?

EMOTIONS AND HORMONES

HORMONE	EMOTION
DOPAMINE • Part of the reward system, or process in the brain that attributes an event with a positive reward like happiness. • Increases motivation and concentration. Healthy Boosting: Healthy diet, creative activities, protected sunlight exposure, Accomplishing goals Unhealthy Boosting: Drug/alcohol use, excessive social media use, risky behaviors (i.e., reckless driving harm to oneself)	
SEROTONIN • Helps with learning and memory • Helps regulate mood, making us feel emotionally stable, happier, and calmer. Healthy Boosting: Adequate sleep, acts of kindness, socializing, expressing gratitude, mindfulness Unhealthy Boosting: Over-reliance on social media for validation, overeating, drug/alcohol use	
ENDORPHINS • Help reduce stress by promoting relaxation • Plays a role in social bonding and connections • Acts as a natural painkiller and induces feelings of happiness and well-being. Healthy Boosting: Exercise, hugs, Spending time in nature, dancing Unhealthy Boosting: Compulsive shopping, violence, risky sexual behaviors, bullying	

EMOTIONS AND HORMONES

HORMONE	EMOTION
OXYTOCIN • Helps with social bonding and is linked to feelings of trust • Has a calming effect, reducing stress and anxiety levels • Linked to altruism and generosity **Healthy Boosting:** Social interaction, laughter, pet interaction **Unhealthy Boosting:** Risky sexual behaviors, unhealthy relationships	
CORTISOL • Helps the body cope with stress by increasing alertness and energy levels. • Plays a role in memory and learning. **Healthy Boosting:** Exercise, healthy nutrition, outdoor activities **Unhealthy Boosting:** Prolonged negatively charged emotions, lack of sleep, overexercising	
ADRENALINE (EPINEPHRINE) • Ignites the fight or flight response • Increases alertness, attention, and focus to help respond to stressful situations. **Healthy Boosting:** Roller coasters, concerts, confronting fears **Unhealthy Boosting:** Violent behaviors, excessive caffeine intake, dangerous stunts	
NOREPINEPHRINE • Works with Adrenaline to ignite the fight or flight response • Bursts of this can lead to happiness **Healthy Boosting:** Cold plunges, goal setting, practicing stress skills **Unhealthy Boosting:** Intense anger or aggression, self-harm, over exerting the body	

What happens if we have too much or too little of these hormones?

Hormone	Too Much	Too Little
Dopamine	Poor impulse control, aggression, and addiction.	Depression, anhedonia (i.e., loss of the ability to feel pleasure), and poor motivation
Serotonin	Agitation, restlessness, confusion.	Depression and hopelessness
Endorphin	Risky behaviors, mood swings, sleeping difficulties, changes in appetite	Reduced stress tolerance, anhedonia, sleeping difficulties, depression
Oxytocin	Difficulty bonding and connection, reduced empathy and trust, depression, and social anxiety	Overattachment, aggression, anxiety, gullibility
Cortisol	Anxiety, depression, slower recovery from exercise, irritability	Fatigue, irritability, anxiety, depression
Adrenaline (Epinephrine)	Adverse health outcomes (i.e., irregular heartbeat and headaches)	Depression, lack of energy
Norepinephrine	High blood pressure, rapid or irregular heart beat, severe headache	Lack of concentration, depression, lethargy

Chronic stress can lead to hormone imbalance and consequences like those described above. We will provide tools that help boost the happiness hormones and decrease the stress hormones, but it's also important to note that hormones can become out of whack due to various medical and mental health conditions that you do not have control over, so if you feel off, always talk to your doctor.

YOUR BRAIN AND EMOTIONS

Emotions originate and are processed in the brain, particularly in the limbic system, which includes structures like the amygdala, hippocampus, and hypothalamus. These regions play a crucial role in generating and regulating emotions.

THE UPSTAIRS AND DOWNSTAIRS BRAIN

The brain is an incredible organ, and while it's complex, we can break it down into two parts to make it easier to understand. Imagine your brain as a two-story house with an upstairs and a downstairs. The stairs connect these two parts.

Let's start by going downstairs to your "reptilian" brain. This part is all about survival instincts, like fight, flight, freeze, or fawn. Here, you experience strong primary emotions like anger, sadness, and fear. These emotions can be intense and powerful.

Now, let's go back up the stairs to the upstairs brain. This part is responsible for more complex actions, such as making good decisions and forming strong friendships. It's also where you feel positive emotions like happiness, excitement, and joy, which are necessary for building hope!

So, think of your brain as a house with an upstairs and a downstairs. Each floor has its own important functions and emotions. Understanding this can help you make sense of your emotions and actions.

Upstairs Brain

Downstairs Brain

You cannot be in the upstairs brain and downstairs brain at the same time.

This is super important because it means that when you're feeling super scared or mad, you're actually in your "downstairs brain." When you're in this mode, your body goes into survival mode, and you instinctively react by fighting, running away, freezing, or even trying to please others (weird, right?).

Now, that's OK if you're facing a life-or-death situation, but it's not so great when it comes to your everyday life. Imagine your teacher drops a surprise quiz on you, and you feel a rush of fear or anger. Your downstairs brain might tell you to flip your desk (fight response), bolt out of the classroom (flight response), or just give up and not even bother (fear response). But, none of those options are gonna help you out.

But fear not! Your "upstairs brain" is here to save the day. It's got all the cool tools you need to handle everyday situations like a champ. Instead of freaking out, your upstairs brain might remind you that you did your homework and you're totally prepared for the quiz (cue positive vibes).

The upstairs brain can also tell you that you're smart enough to tackle those tough problems if you use what you know (hello, problem-solving skills). Plus, it's easier to think clearly and come up with answers when you're not stuck in your downstairs brain.

So, understanding the difference between your upstairs and downstairs brain is key to handling your emotions in a healthy way. It's like having a secret superpower that helps you respond to tough situations like a pro.

Labeling the Upstairs and Downstairs Brain

Upstairs Brain

Downstairs Brain

WORD BANK: *Anger, Fear, Relaxed, Happy, Sadness, Excited*

GROUP DISCUSSION

☀ *Why do we call the emotions in the downstairs brain negatively charged emotions? What do you think happens if we stay in the downstairs brain for too long?*

☀ *What part of the brain causes us to make bad decisions (i.e., using substances, engaging in aggressive behaviors?)*

☀ *Where do we access hope?*

EMOTIONS AND YOUR BODY

Emotions aren't just in your brain—they can affect your body too. When you experience emotions, you might notice changes in your body like a faster heartbeat, tense muscles, or a warm feeling. It's because your brain and body are connected, and they work together to make you feel and react to different situations. So, emotions are not just something happening in your head; they're a whole-body experience.

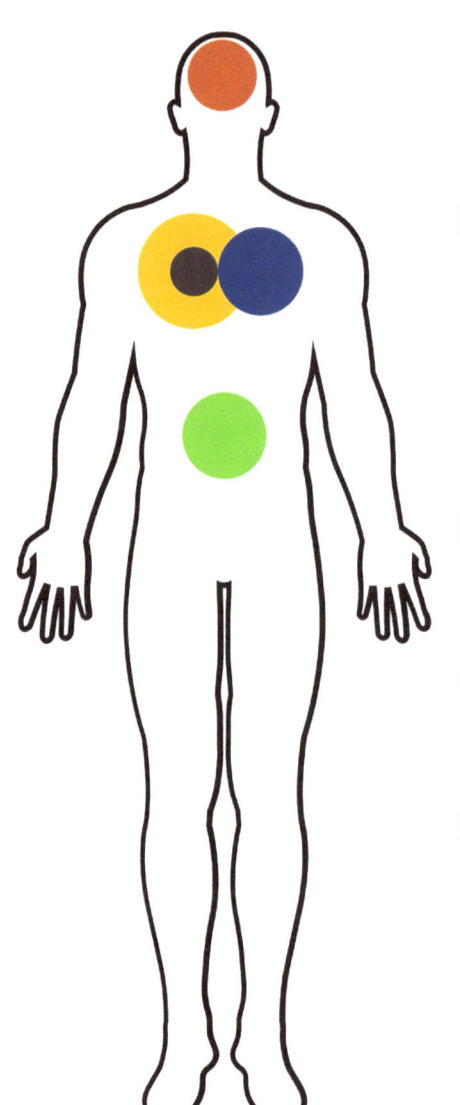

Anger
Sense of tension and heat in body, muscles tighten and may feel a surge of energy or restlessness

Fear
Racing heart, sweaty palms, knot in your stomach

Happiness
Warm pleasant sensation in your chest or lightless in your body

Sadness
Feels heavy and constructing. Sinking feeling in chest, tears in eyes, general sense of fatigue

Excitement
Tends to create a buzz of energy throughout the body. You might feel a quickening heartbeat, butterflies in your stomach, or a tingling sensation. Your body might feel more alert and ready for action.

Recognizing how our body feels during different emotions is crucial. Often, our body sends signals before our mind realizes how we're feeling. By paying attention to these physical signs, we can actively shift from reacting impulsively (using the downstairs brain) to thinking logically (using our upstairs brain), which might help decrease feelings of despair and helplessness.

Exploring where you feel emotions. In the blank people cutouts below, label the primary emotions and color in where you feel them in your body.

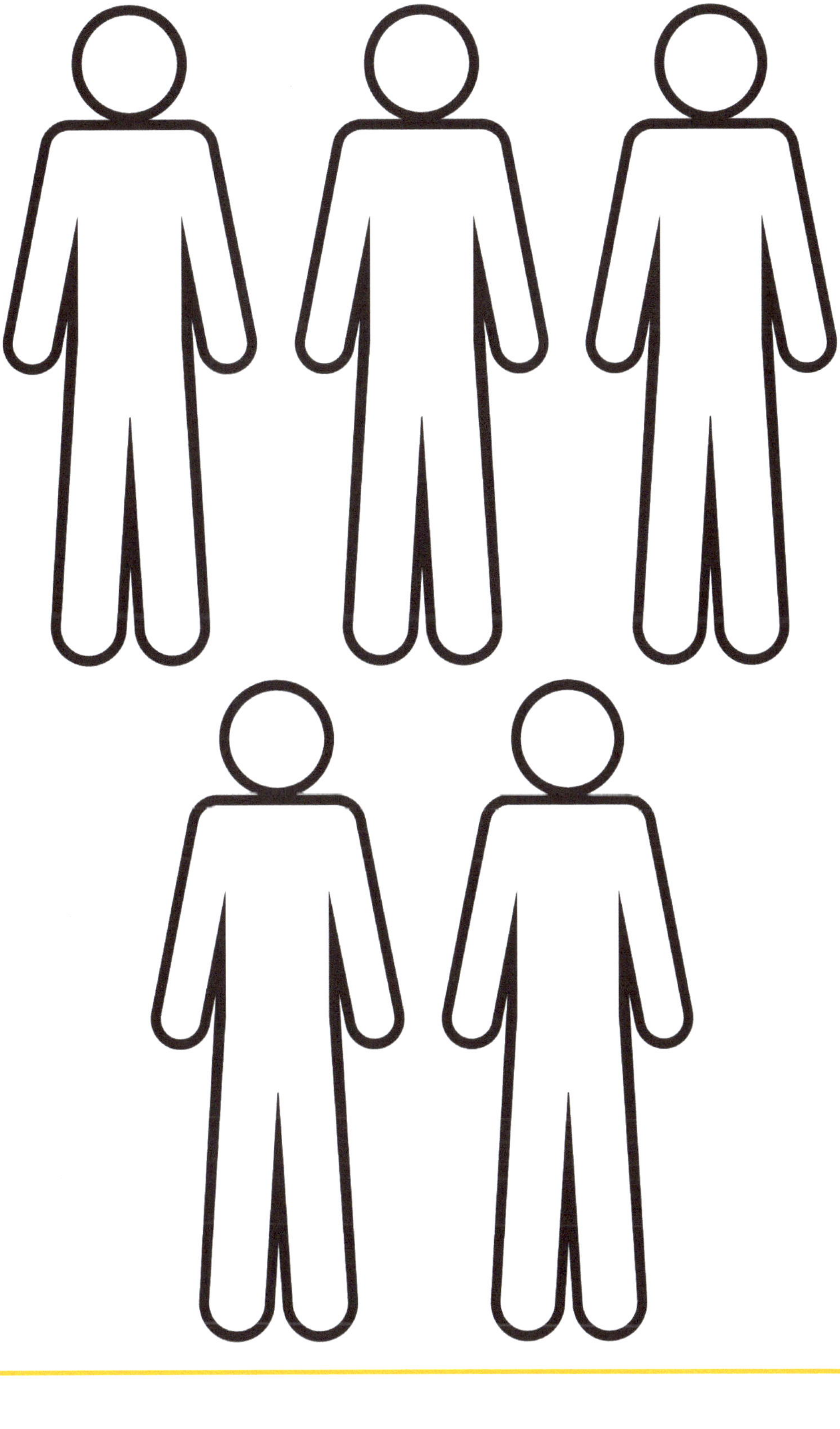

☀ *Share your people and discuss where you feel emotions. Are there differences between the group members?*

Now, you might be wondering how you can shift from your downstairs brain to your upstairs brain, or how to stay in your upstairs brain. Don't worry, this Hopeguide is here to help! It will provide you with the tools you need to take control of your emotions and manage your downstairs brain more effectively.

YOUR BRAIN, YOUR EMOTIONS, AND HOPE: TYING EVERYTHING TOGETHER

Hope is often fueled by positively charged emotions such as relaxation, excitement, and happiness. When we experience these positively charged emotions, it enhances our sense of hope and belief in the possibilities that lie ahead. These emotions create a fertile ground for hope to thrive, motivating us to set goals, take action, and work towards a better future.

On the other hand, negatively charged emotions such as fear, sadness, or anger can challenge our hope and make it harder to envision a positive future. When we are overwhelmed by negatively charged emotions, it can be challenging to maintain hope or see a way out of difficult circumstances.

When you notice yourself in the downstairs brain, you can take action to move to the upstairs brain.

GROUP DISCUSSION

☀ *What is an action you can take for the following situations if you notice that you are in your downstairs brain?*

- *Receiving a bad grade*
- *Overhearing that people are talking about you*
- *Being cut off in traffic*
- *Giving the wrong answer in front of the class*
- *Going through a break-up*

GROUP ACTIVITY

Acting Out Emotions

1. *Split into pairs and choose one of the scenarios below. Create a skit about the scenario in which you respond with either your upstairs or downstairs brain. Once you perform your skit, have the rest of the group answer the following questions:*
   a. *Which section of the brain did you and your partner react with during the skit?*
   b. *What emotions were you and your partner feeling during the skit?*
   c. *What is another way that this scenario could have played out?*

2. *Scenarios:*
   a. *You get to class in the morning and your teacher tells the class that there is a surprise test.*
   b. *You come home to find out that your least favorite food is being served for dinner.*
   c. *You find out your friend lied to you.*
   d. *Someone stole something of yours.*
   e. *Someone accidentally bumps into you in the hallway.*
   f. *Your school decides that everyone should wear suits as part of the new dress code.*

LADY GAGA

Pop icon Lady Gaga (Stefani Joanne Germanotta) is celebrated for her bold fashion choices and eccentric style. However, when she was younger, these traits made her the target of the school bullies. Bullies teased her, put her in trash cans, and called her derogatory names. When she went to NYU, some of her classmates even created a "Stefani Germanotta, you'll never be famous" Facebook group.

Imagine all the negatively charged emotions she must have felt. Lady Gaga has said, "I felt a tremendous amount of stress, a tremendous amount of anxiety, isolation. I felt lonely, I felt misunderstood. I felt stupid even thought I was smart." Luckily, she didn't give in to those negatively charged emotions. She knew she couldn't control the bullies, so she instead controlled her mindset and how she managed her emotions.

Lady Gaga took pauses when she was bullied to breathe deeply, meditate, and listen to what her feelings were telling her. She then expressed those feelings the only way she knew how: through her music.

Lady Gaga would not be the famous singer she is today if she didn't have the skills to overcome and speak openly about the way her bullies made her feel. Like Lady Gaga, we can use Stress Skills to turn adversity into inspiration and hopelessness into hope.*

This story was created from publicly available information. It does not suggest endorsement of Hopeful Minds, or any affiliation by known celebrity to our program. All information is for illustrative purposes for youth, to demonstrate skills used to create, maintain, and grow hope.

☀ *What is one piece of information you found most helpful in this lesson?*

☀ *How will you incorporate the information you learned in this lesson to your life this week?*

☀ *What is your most challenging emotion? Brainstorm strategies to manage it.*

☀ *Lady Gaga talks about all the emotions she felt in school; what has been your experience with negatively charged emotions?*

WEEKLY HOPE ACTIVATION

Inspired Actions for Hope are the things you can do to reinforce these lessons and begin to bring hope skills into your daily life. Choose at least one of the actions below to complete before moving on from this lesson.

☀ **Using art can be a great way to help you identify your emotions.**
Take 10 minutes to draw the emotions you are currently feeling. Use colors, shapes, words, or designs to depict each emotion.

☀ **Emotional Check-In Journaling:**
Each day write down a few of the emotions you felt during the day and how you recognize that you felt that emotion. Use the sunflower emotion wheel to help you identify the emotion words.

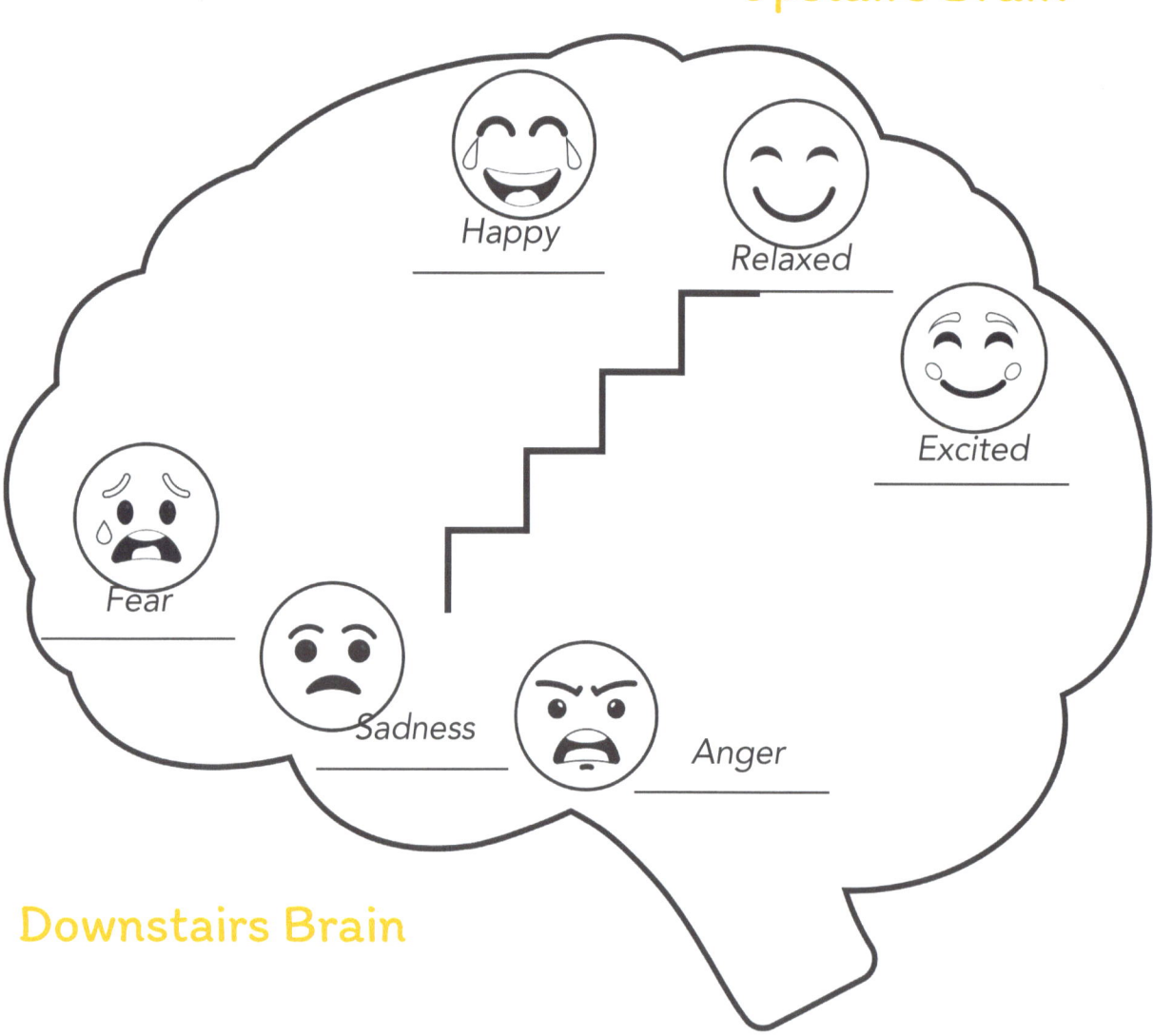

Upstairs Brain

Happy

Relaxed

Excited

Fear

Sadness

Anger

Downstairs Brain

NOTES

Post your completed activities on social media using the following hashtags to help us teach the lessons. Make sure to tag us **@ifredorg** and **@theshinehopecompany.**

#HopefulMindsTeens #Hope #ShineHope #ScienceofHope #BrainAndEmotion #EmotionsAndHormone #Shine

SHINE HOPE™
A HOW-TO FOR HOPE IN TRYING TIMES

Scan to download the clickable version of this infographic

STRESS SKILLS	**H**APPINESS HABITS	**I**NSPIRED ACTIONS	**N**OURISHING NETWORKS	**E**LIMINATING CHALLENGES
90 second pause	Activating purpose	WOOP process	5:1 Rule	Limiting beliefs
Belly breathing	Pursuing passion	SMART goals	Compassion	Automatic Negative Thoughts (ANTs)
Journaling	Utilizing strengths	Stretch goals	Forgiveness	All-or-nothing thinking
Gardening	Meditation	Achievement goals	Love	Negative bias
Calming music	Smiling	Intrinsic goals	Gratitude	Rumination & Worry
Affirming beliefs	Exercising / Nutrition	Mastery goals	Recognition	Focusing on Uncontrollables
Sensory engagement	Creating / listening to music	Micro goals / Stepping	Support	Attaching to outcomes
Cold plunge	Dancing / Singing	Habit Stacking	Faith	Internalizing failure
Decluttering	Drawing / Painting	Visualization	Trust	Toxic Consumption
Prayer	Gratitude	Overcoming obstacles	Respect	Nocebo Effect
Nature walk	Volunteering	Regoaling	Effective Listening	Mind Wandering
Napping	Wonder / Awe	Write down goals / check in	Empathy	Implicit Bias
Laughter	Quality sleep		Kindness	Negative Framing
Crying	Doodling		Animals	Perfectionism
Tapping				Taking things personally
Yoga				
Mantras				

the shine hope™ company

© The Shine Hope Company, LLC

Scan the QR Code to measure hope with the Hope Scale!

Module 4:
The First Key to Shine Hope: Stress Skills

Module 4: The First Key to Shine Hope: Stress Skills

Stress skills, the "S" in Shine, are skills that help you manage negatively charged emotions. We often experience negatively charged emotions during moments of hopelessness, and it's important to develop strategies to managing those emotions to help cultivate hope.

THE HOPE MATRIX CONNECTION

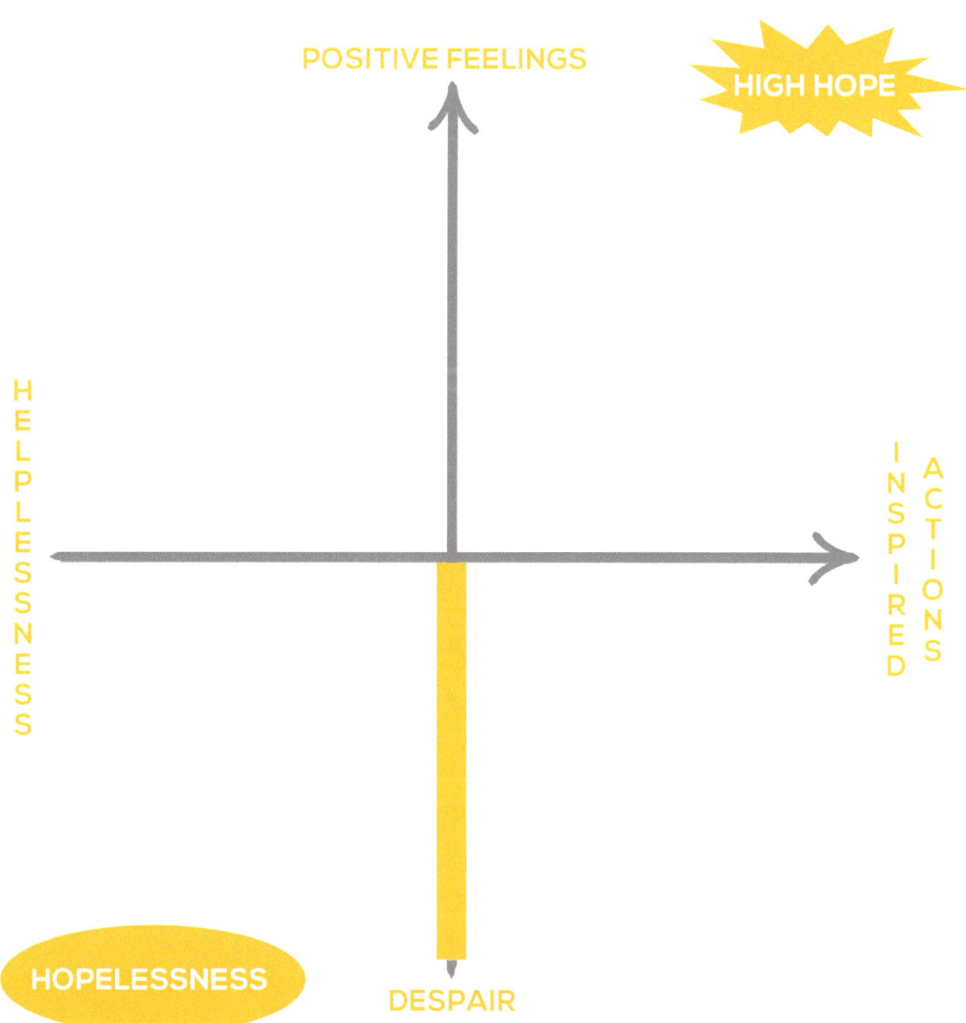

We all experience stress, it's entirely normal. Experts[1] believe we need a certain amount of stress to function at an optimum level because stress motivates us to make changes and reach our goals.

However, persistent stress leads to many negative consequences that can have a lasting effect on our overall health and well-being; this is called the allostatic load. We experience the allostatic load when the challenges we face in our environment exceed our ability to cope.

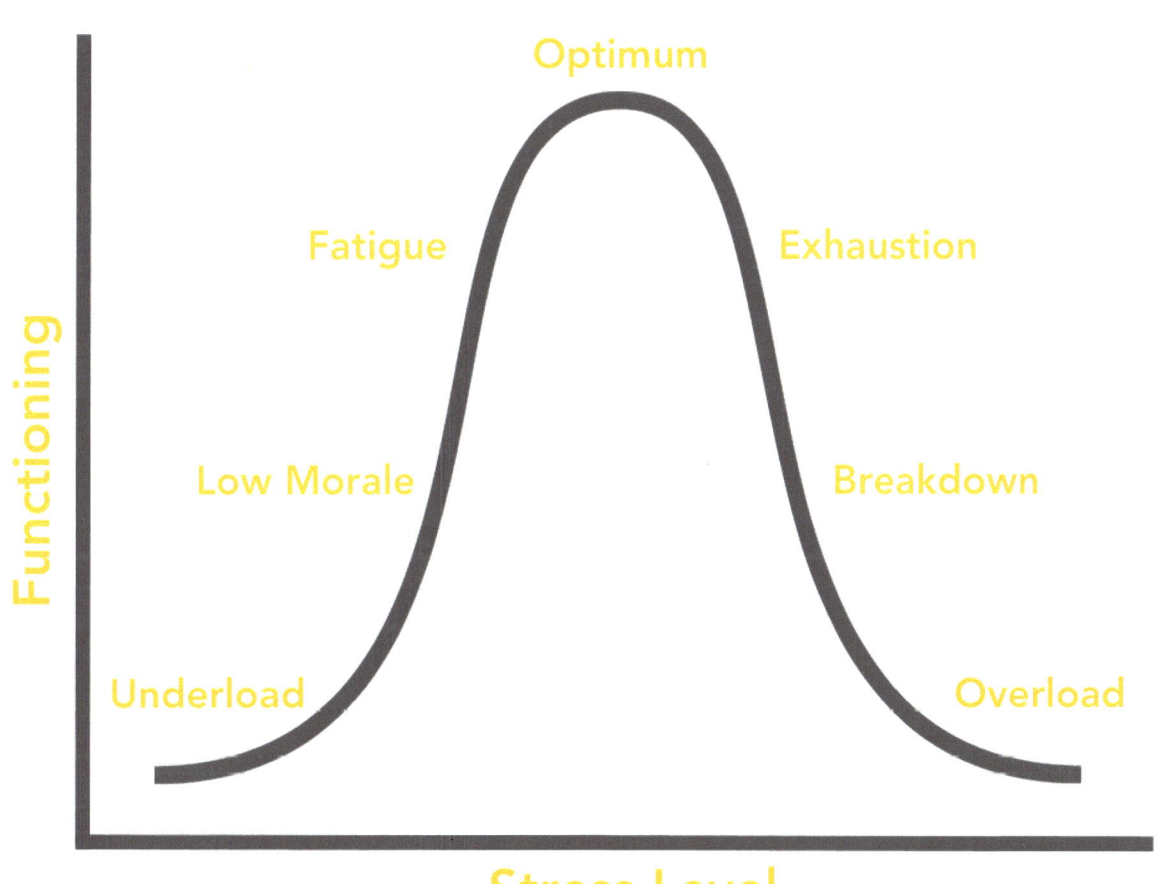

GROUP DISCUSSION

☀ *How can you tell whether the stress you are feeling is healthy or allostatic load? (Hint: Think about how your body feels)*

[1] *news.berkeley.edu/2013/04/16/researchers-find-out-why-some-stress-is-good-for-you/*

THE STRESS RESPONSE

What happens to our brain when we face stress? When you are triggered by something in your environment, such as an upcoming test, tryouts, or a new social situation, your brain releases stress hormones that force you into your downstairs brain. This is called your stress response.

The biology behind your stress response can be explained by Dr. Jill Bolte Taylor's 90-second rule. For 90 seconds after the environmental trigger, your body is flooded with stress hormones (i.e., adrenaline, cortisol, and norepinephrine), and it becomes nearly impossible to return to the upstairs brain in that first 90 seconds because of the biological response that your body is going through.

Too much of the stress hormones have a few important impacts on the brain, including:

- Depleted dopamine (the happy hormone), which can decrease motivation.

- Increases the risk of developing anxiety or depression.

- Increased risk of aggression, even if the stress hormone spiked for reasons not related to aggression. *(Once someone has acted aggressively as a result of stress hormones, they are more likely to become violent in the future when faced with stress)*

However, if no additional environmental stimulation occurs, the stress chemical process ends after 90 seconds. This means that once the 90 seconds are complete, you have the power to decide whether you want to stay in your downstairs brain or return to your upstairs brain.

 Any emotional response after 90 seconds is a result of your choice.

Your ability to learn to control the stress response proactively is the First Key to Shine Hope because it is what empowers you to start controlling how you react to triggers in your environment. During this time in your life, you may experience many hormone shifts that can keep you in the downstairs brain, and unfortunately, this is a very normal experience (although it doesn't feel very good!)

Developing ways to manage stress now will greatly impact how you feel physically and emotionally. It will also help you develop and maintain healthy relationships with people around you.

One great first step to managing stress is to think about what triggers stress in your life. Then, ask yourself, are you controlling the triggers, or are they controlling you? It is by learning how to control these triggers you can get back to your upstairs brain.

GROUP ACTIVITY

Below is a list of common stressors or triggers. Your task is to indicate how you typically respond to at least 5 of the stressors, both behaviorally and emotionally. Think about how you react when faced with these stressors. You can provide brief descriptions or keywords for your responses.

Exams or tests

Public speaking

Conflicts with friends

Family arguments

Time management

Relationship breakups	
Changes or transitions	
College or job loss	
Body image concerns	
Bullying	
Peer pressure	

 You reacting to someone else that triggers you gives them your power. Take your power back by learning how to manage your stress.

 **GROUP DISCUSSION**

☀ *What are other things that cause you stress? What happens when you experience stress?*

☀ *How does stress impact your mental and physical health?*

STRESS SKILLS

Stress Skills are the skills that help you navigate your 90-second physiological response, manage your stress response, and re-enter your upstairs brain. They allow you to manage the emotional despair found in hopelessness and move towards positive feelings and hope.

When we experience stress, our body releases elevated levels of cortisol, epinephrine, and norepinephrine. These increased stress hormones can sometimes drive us towards engaging in unhealthy activities as an attempt to alleviate the stress. Such activities may include:

- Ignoring or denying stress
- Becoming isolated or withdrawn
- Using substances
- Procrastinating or avoiding responsibilities

- Talking negatively to self
- Self-harm
- Aggression or anger outbursts
- Neglecting one's health

What are some examples of unhealthy ways to manage stress?

When you use unhealthy ways to deal with stress, it may feel like a temporary relief because happy hormones like dopamine are released, which gives us a brief sense of pleasure or distraction. However, these coping mechanisms do not address the root causes of stress and can actually make things worse, keeping you in the downstairs brain.

Instead of resorting to unhealthy ways of dealing with stress, it's crucial to focus on developing healthy stress skills. These skills are like superpowers that help you handle your emotions after that initial 90-second stress response. They guide you towards using your "upstairs brain," which is responsible for clear thinking and making safe choices.

By building healthy stress skills, you can take care of your well-being, stay in control, and avoid getting caught up in aggressive behaviors that you wouldn't normally engage in. These skills empower you to handle stress in a positive way, making you stronger and more balanced emotionally.

There are two types of healthy Stress Skills: **Short-term and long-term Stress Skills.**

SHORT-TERM STRESS SKILLS

Short-term Stress Skills are quick actions that you can take to navigate your 90-second stress response. They include actions such as:

- Taking a 90-Second Pause (The Clear Button)
- Deep breathing
- Being aware of the feelings and leaning into them
- Listening to calming music
- Tapping
- Engaging your five senses to get present
- Going for a walk

LONG-TERM STRESS SKILLS

Long-term Stress Skills are skills you can practice that help you alleviate chronic stress or train your mind and body to better respond to triggers. They include actions such as:

- Consistently practicing Mindfulness Meditation
- Spending time in nature
- Visualizing
- Writing in a journal
- Talking to a trusted friend or adult, or therapist
- Helping someone else
- Any other actions that help you manage your stress
- Exercise/sports
- Creative Expression (i.e., *drawing/coloring/ music, writing, building, etc.*)

BELLY BREATHING PRACTICE

Deep breathing is one of the most important Stress Skills that we can use. If you want to have really strong hope, it's important to practice deep breathing 2-3 times each day. *(Check out Goal Meditation Music at Page 196)*

Belly breathing instructions:

- Sit in a comfortable position with your back as straight as possible.
- Notice how your body feels. Take a few seconds to just relax. Relax your neck, shoulders, arms, legs, and feet. Can you feel your heartbeat? Can you sense your breath? Try a few big exhales.
- When you're ready, place one hand on your chest and the other on your belly button (below the rib cage).
- Now take a long, slow, deep breath in through your nose for a count of 10 (or as long as you are able). As you breathe in, you want to send the air to your belly button. Your hand on your belly should rise while the hand on your chest remains still.
- Once you get to 10, slowly exhale out of your mouth. Feel the muscles of your stomach tighten and your hand lower.

Do this for at least 90 seconds (or 10 slow, deep breaths). How do you feel after deep breathing? Do you feel any different?

Another excellent short-term Stress Skill is completing a puzzle, such as a word search, because it is a low-stake activity and they're fun!

They also force your mind to focus on the present moment; if you are someone who struggles with an overly active mind, then this can be an activity that forces you to be in the moment, which may settle your thoughts. Try the one below to practice a short-term Stress Skill.

Stress Skill Word Search

```
q d d v p v f a p e l n c x b
l j o m e a g t b t r a o p r
q s b u s x p q u e v t l t e
y t h s k k a o q m j u o h a
e a p i u o k j f j o r r y t
v l i c b f w q c t i e i t h
p k q q w w n b t x u p n n i
e i f i v e s e n s e s g h n
x n i z b f c z w r i t i n g
e g r l f w n e v e p q t s u
r q k k m z d s e o y m r k y
c h e l p i n g o t h e r s f
i o x f s m c q y k t y w r h
s a u p e h t v h p n j r i l
e w g m m i n d f u l n e s s
```

WORD BANK

Helping others

mindfulness

five senses

Coloring

exercise

writing

Breathing

talking

nature

Music

GROUP ACTIVITY

Matching Activity.

Your task is to match each stress management skill with its corresponding category, either "Unhealthy" or "Healthy."

	HEALTHY	UNHEALTHY
Intentionally isolation yourself from others		
Engaging in physical exercise		
Procrastinating on tasks		
Seeking support from friends or family		
Using drugs or alcohol to numb feelings		
Practicing deep breathing and relaxation techniques		
Venting frustrations through aggressive behavior		
Talking to a trusted adult or counselor		
Being mean to a friend		
Snapping at your sibling		
Overreacting to a situation		
Smoking cigarettes or vaping		
Practicing mindfulness		
Drinking alcohol		
Starting physical fights		
Joining a club		
Getting out for a walk		

MOOD TRACKER

Directions: Practice different Stress Skills and notice your emotion following the Stress Skills. Additionally, monitor your nightly sleep duration, the time spent on physical activity or sports, and your overall nutrition for the day. Take note of your emotions throughout the day in relation to these factors. Keep this tracker to help determine what skills work best for you.

STRESS SKILL	MOOD AFTER USING STRESS SKILL
	😀 🙂 😐 🙁 ☹️ 😫
	😀 🙂 😐 🙁 ☹️ 😫
	😀 🙂 😐 🙁 ☹️ 😫
	😀 🙂 😐 🙁 ☹️ 😫
NIGHTLY SLEEP DURATION	
	😀 🙂 😐 🙁 ☹️ 😫
	😀 🙂 😐 🙁 ☹️ 😫
	😀 🙂 😐 🙁 ☹️ 😫
	😀 🙂 😐 🙁 ☹️ 😫
TIME SPENT ON PHYSICAL ACTIVITY/SPORTS	
	😀 🙂 😐 🙁 ☹️ 😫
	😀 🙂 😐 🙁 ☹️ 😫
	😀 🙂 😐 🙁 ☹️ 😫
	😀 🙂 😐 🙁 ☹️ 😫
OVERALL NUTRITION	
	😀 🙂 😐 🙁 ☹️ 😫
	😀 🙂 😐 🙁 ☹️ 😫
	😀 🙂 😐 🙁 ☹️ 😫
	😀 🙂 😐 🙁 ☹️ 😫

As you begin to practice Stress Skills, keep track of which ones you like and don't like in the area below:

What short-term Stress Skills work for you when you are in your stress response?

What long-term Stress Skills work best for managing your stress?

STRESS SKILLS AND HOPE:
TYING EVERYTHING TOGETHER

Managing stress is vital for fostering and maintaining hope in our lives. When we're overwhelmed by stress, it can make us feel anxious and have moments of hopelessness, but by actively managing stress, we protect our emotional well-being and create room for hope to grow. Stress management techniques help us cope with challenges and setbacks, allowing us to stay resilient and positive. When we effectively manage stress, it clears our minds, enabling us to think clearly and find solutions to problems.

MICHELLE OBAMA

Michelle Obama is known as many things: an author, lawyer, philanthropist, mother, public speaker, and the first African American First Lady of the United States. But what you might not know is that she is also a Hope Hero and a master of Stress Skills.

At many times throughout her life, including when she was the First Lady of the United States, Michelle has suffered bullying and discrimination. When Michelle is faced with sexism and racism, she says that the first thing she does is to "take a deep breath."

She uses her anger as wisdom, and it informs her on what she cares about. After she breaths and gets to her upstairs brain, she says 'What can I DO to create change', and then she uses her power to take inspired action and make change.

She knows that she cannot control the opinions and discrimination of the people around her. What she can control is how she reacts to them. Michelle uses her deep breathing to return to her upstairs brain, and then follows her mantra: "When they go low, I go high." When other people address her with their downstairs brain, she makes sure to respond with her upstairs brain.

Like Michelle, we can all learn to deep belly breathe when we are triggered so that we can respond to stressful situations from our upstairs brain. And, like Michelle, we can use our hope skills to "go high," even when others "go low."*

This story was created from publicly available information. It does not suggest endorsement of Hopeful Minds, or any affiliation by known celebrity to our program. All information is for illustrative purposes for youth, to demonstrate skills used to create, maintain, and grow hope.

☀ *What are your favorite stress skills?*

☀ *What is one piece of information you found most helpful in this lesson?*

☀ *How will you incorporate the information you learned in this lesson to your life this week?*

☀ *Michelle Obama used numerous Stress Skills when faced with sexism and racism. With permission, search online to see if you can find other Stress Skills Michelle used that weren't outlined in the Hope Hero Spotlight.*

Go back to the very first worksheet on page 11, where you identified your hope hero. Fill in the Stress Skills your hope hero has used when facing negatively charged emotions.

WEEKLY HOPE ACTIVATION

Inspired Actions for Hope are the things you can do to reinforce these lessons and begin to bring hope skills into your daily life. Choose at least one of the actions below to complete before moving to the next lesson.

☀ Use the blank Bingo card below to play Stress Skills Bingo. Have each person in the group fill out the Bingo card with Stress Skills they plan to practice in the upcoming week. During the week, mark off a square when you've practiced the Stress Skill. At the start of the next group meeting, take turns talking about the stress skills group members practiced and see who achieved Bingo!

☀ When we have a lot to do, it can cause us to feel overwhelmed and activate our stress response. Sometimes the simple act of writing down all of the tasks we have on our minds helps to alleviate stress. It is especially helpful to do this before bed so that our mind is calm before we sleep. Take a few minutes to journal about the things that are currently stressful in your life.

☀ Complete the mood tracker to see what Stress Skills are useful for you.

STRESS SKILLS
BINGO

Stress Skill Word Search

```
q  d  d  v  p  v  f  a  p  e  l  n  c  x  b
l  j  o  m  e  a  g  t  b  t  r  a  o  p  r
q  s  b  u  s  x  p  q  u  e  v  t  l  t  e
y  t  h  s  k  k  a  o  q  m  j  u  o  h  a
e  a  p  i  u  o  k  j  f  j  o  r  r  y  t
v  l  i  c  b  f  w  q  c  t  i  e  i  t  h
p  k  q  q  w  w  n  b  t  x  u  p  n  n  i
e  i  f  i  v  e  s  e  n  s  e  s  g  h  n
x  n  i  z  b  f  c  z  w  r  i  t  i  n  g
e  g  r  l  f  w  n  e  v  e  p  q  t  s  u
r  q  k  k  m  z  d  s  e  o  y  m  r  k  y
c  h  e  l  p  i  n  g  o  t  h  e  r  s  f
i  o  x  t  s  m  c  q  y  k  t  y  w  r  h
s  a  u  p  e  h  t  v  h  p  n  j  r  i  l
e  w  g  m  m  i  n  d  f  u  l  n  e  s  s
```

WORD BANK

Helping others	mindfulness	five senses
Coloring	exercise	writing
Breathing	talking	nature
Music		

Answer Keys:

	HEALTHY	UNHEALTHY
Intentionally isolation yourself from others		X
Engaging in physical exercise	X	
Procrastinating on tasks		X
Seeking support from friends or family	X	
Using drugs or alcohol to numb feelings		X
Practicing deep breathing and relaxation techniques	X	
Venting frustrations through aggressive behavior		X
Talking to a trusted adult or counselor	X	
Being mean to a friend		X
Snapping at your sibling		X
Overreacting to a situation		X
Smoking cigarettes or vaping		X
Practicing mindfulness	X	
Drinking alcohol		X
Starting physical fights		X
Joining a club	X	
Getting out for a walk	X	

NOTES

Post your completed activities on social media using the following hashtags to help us teach the lessons. Make sure to tag us **@ifredorg** and **@theshinehopecompany.**

#HopefulMindsTeens #Hope #ShineHope #ScienceofHope
#StressSkills #StressResponse #BellyBreathing #90SecondRule

STRESS SKILLS

Stress Skills are actions that help you navigate your stress response and work through your body's chemical response to external stimuli. By practicing them, you are teaching yourself how to proactively manage the emotional despair found in hopelessness and move towards positive feelings where you activate hope.

The Stress Response

This is when you are emotionally triggered by something in your environment, and you go into fight, flight, freeze, or fawn mode as your body releases stress hormones, such as cortisol, adrenaline, and norepinephrine. You are in your downstairs brain, and can't reach your upstairs brain; the upstairs brain is the place where you make good decisions for moving towards all you hope for in life.

90 second pause	Sensory engagement	Laughter
Belly breathing	Cold plunge	Crying
Journaling	Decluttering	Tapping
Gardening	Prayer	Yoga
Calming music	Nature walk	Mantras
Affirming beliefs	Napping	

Module 5:
The Second Key to S**h**ine Hope: <u>H</u>appiness Habits

Module 5: The Second Key to Shine Hope: Happiness Habits

Happiness Habits, the "H" in Shine, are skills that help maintain positive feelings. We are less likely to experience lasting negatively charged emotions if we consistently practice the Happiness Habits that keep up in the upstairs brain.

THE HOPE MATRIX CONNECTION

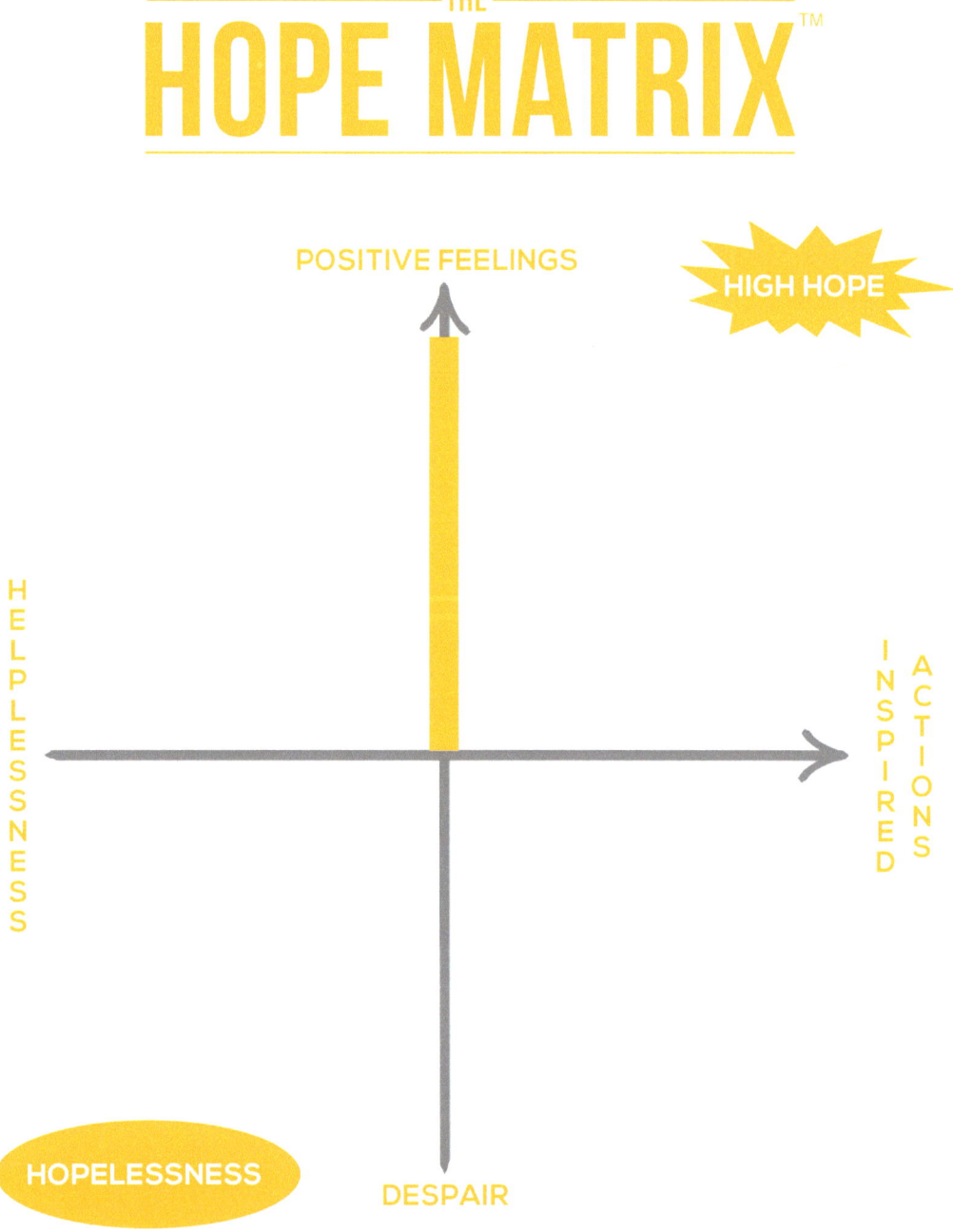

The Second Key to Shine Hope is Fostering Happiness Habits.

Happiness Habits are healthy, long-term actions that you can take to foster positive feelings and stay in your upstairs brain. In other words, they are the activities you consistently engage in to maintain positive feelings.

Positive feelings are the feelings that help you cultivate hope and encourage you to keep moving toward your goals. If you want to have a strong hopeful mindset, you want to spend as much time as possible in your upstairs brain.

When you perform your Happiness Habits, your brain releases happiness hormones, including endorphins, dopamine, serotonin, and oxytocin. When these chemicals are released, you experience increased levels of happiness, which in turn fosters positive feelings. When you maintain daily Happiness Habits, you are ensuring future happiness and hope.

Stress Skills

Happiness Habits

Positive Feelings

Help to quickly move from downstairs brain to upstairs brain; combats cortisol that's released in times of stress.

- Used in times of stress
- An Intervention when you feel stress
- Can provide relief from the stress
- **TIP: Remember the 90-second response**

Help keep in upstairs brain & your brain releases happiness hormones, including endorphins, dopamine, serotonin, and oxytocin. When these chemicals are released, you experience increased levels of happiness.

- Used all the time
- A prevention against stress
- Can help maintain positive emotions
- **TIP: Remember to practice Happiness Habits regularly**

Coloring in this Venn diagram is a Happiness Habit!

HAPPINESS HABITS AND HORMONES

Think back to Module 3 of this hopeguide; the hormones related to happiness are dopamine, serotonin, endorphin, and oxytocin.

Hormone	Healthy way to induce it	Unhealthy way to induce it
Dopamine	<ul><li>Healthy diet</li><li>Creative activities</li><li>Protected sunlight exposure</li><li>Accomplishing goals</li></ul>	<ul><li>Drug/alcohol use</li><li>Excessive social media use</li><li>Risky behaviors (*i.e., reckless driving harm to oneself*)</li></ul>
Serotonin	<ul><li>Adequate sleep</li><li>Acts of kindness</li><li>Socializing</li><li>Expressing gratitude</li><li>Mindfulness</li></ul>	<ul><li>Over-reliance on social media for validation</li><li>Overeating</li><li>Drug/alcohol use</li></ul>
Endorphin	<ul><li>Exercise</li><li>Hugs</li><li>Spending time in nature</li><li>Dancing</li></ul>	<ul><li>Compulsive shopping</li><li>Violence</li><li>Risky sexual behaviors</li></ul>
Oxytocin	<ul><li>Social interaction</li><li>Laughter</li><li>Pet interaction</li></ul>	<ul><li>Risky sexual behaviors</li><li>Unhealthy relationships</li></ul>

GROUP DISCUSSION

What are some healthy and unhealthy activities that people do to increase Happiness Hormones?

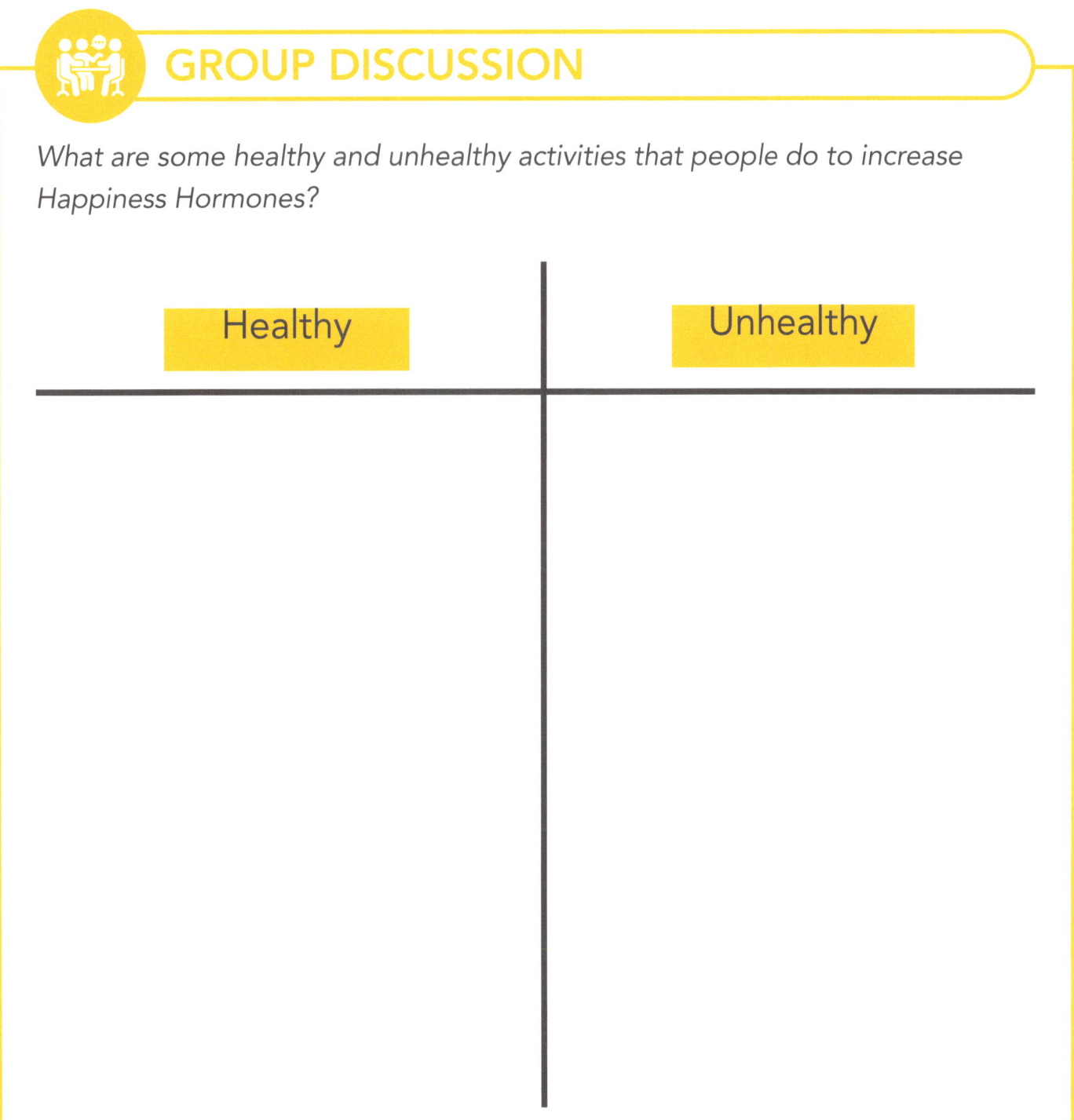

Healthy	Unhealthy

Teens naturally have lower levels of dopamine and are more sensitive to dopamine spikes. This means your brain will likely respond to enjoyable activities more. However, the spike of dopamine also drowns out warning signs that an activity might be dangerous.

Dopamine plays a big role in our brain's reward system, so it's easy to become addicted to unhealthy activities that spike dopamine and make us feel good. However, it's just as easy to develop a passion for a healthy happiness habit.

A great way to induce happiness hormones in a healthy way is through creative expression, such as coloring. Take some time to color the sunflower mandala below for a healthy way to spike your happy hormones.

PRACTICING HAPPINESS HABITS

When we get busy or stressed, we tend to skip our Happiness Habits. Building habits can be hard, and if you fall out of practice, it can be easy to feel discouraged. When we feel discouraged, it's important that we don't turn to unhealthy ways of inducing happy hormones.

Practicing healthy Happiness Habits requires persistence, not perfection; each time you take the time out of your day to practice a healthy Happiness Habit, you are demonstrating a small act of self-compassion that can help you maintain hope.

 **GROUP DISCUSSION**

☀ *How do Happiness Habits make you feel?*

☀ *When is the last time you set aside time to engage in a Happiness Habit?*

☀ *What do you notice about yourself when you haven't engaged in a Happiness Habit in a while?*

☀ *What gets in the way of you practicing Happiness Habits? How can you manage those barriers?*

Sometimes, when life is very busy, it's helpful to schedule your Happiness Habits so that they are integrated into your day without too much extra thought. Continuing to practice Happiness Habits helps us create the habit, as practicing once or twice won't necessarily result in change.

Happiness Habits are incredibly important for your physical and mental health. When you practice healthy, long-term Happiness Habits, they create numerous positive outcomes, including:

IMPROVE CONFIDENCE

IMPROVE SLEEP

IMPROVE ENERGY TO MEET GOALS

REDUCE ANXIETY AND DEPRESSION

IMPROVE MEMORY

IMPROVE HEALTH

The first step in building Happiness Habits is looking after our bodies. This includes getting sufficient sleep, eating nutritious foods, and making sure you exercise regularly. Taking care of your body not only keeps you healthy but also makes it easier to embrace and practice Happiness Habits.

HAPPINESS HABITS

Below are some of our favorite Happiness Habits.

- Setting purposeful goals
- Practicing gratitude
- Acting with kindness
- Thinking about positive things that make us happy
- Exercising
- Eating healthy foods like fruits and vegetables
- Walking outside
- Focusing on faith
- Playing an instrument
- Singing
- Massage

- Experiencing wonder or awe
- Being creative
- Taking photos
- Drawing, painting, or coloring
- Dancing
- Doing jumping jacks
- Skipping
- Listening to happy music
- Spending time with friends
- Volunteering
- Any other positive actions that make you happy

Chances are you already do a couple of these Happiness Habits, even if you haven't called them Happiness Habits until now. For lots of us, our Happiness Habits are the hobbies that we do in our free time that make us happy.

Another one of our favorite Happiness Habits involves using creativity. As a group, practice creativity together with the following game:

THE COLLABORATIVE STORYTELLING GAME

As a group, you will develop a story about Happiness Habits. Designate one person to start the story, then take turns adding a sentence to the story until it is complete. Each person should build upon the sentence from the person before them. Try to be as creative and imaginative when creating part of the story. Humor is strongly encouraged!

HAPPINESS HABITS AND HOPE: TYING EVERYTHING TOGETHER

Happiness and hope are interconnected forces that greatly influence each other. When we experience happiness, it creates a positive environment that nurtures and strengthens our sense of hope. Happiness habits also fuel our resilience and optimism, allowing us to face challenges with determination and the belief that we can overcome them.

Happiness acts as a powerful motivator, inspiring us to set goals, develop strategies, and take action toward achieving them. In turn, as our hopes and aspirations start to materialize, they contribute to our overall happiness and fulfillment. So, by embracing happiness and maintaining a hopeful outlook, we create a continuous cycle of positivity and growth that propels us toward a brighter future.

HOPE HERO SPOTLIGHT

KEANU REEVES

Keanu Reeves is known as one of the most humble, kind, and grateful actors in Hollywood. After all of his success throughout his career, it is easy to see that he has a lot to be thankful for. However, it has been the tragedies, rather than the successes, that have truly taught Keanu gratitude.

Amidst the Hollywood fame, Keanu struggled through the death of a friend, a stillborn child, the death of his wife, and a sister battling leukemia. In these moments, we can only imagine how hard it must have been for Keanu to find things to be grateful for.

Keanu is a testament to the power of hope. His loss and hardships helped him appreciate the small things in life. When he faced hopelessness, he listened to his negative feelings and learned from them, and found Happiness Habits that helped him cultivate hope, such as getting regular exercise through wushi, boxing, krav, maga, and jujitsu.

When you are having a hard time finding things to be grateful for, just remember these words from Keanu: "Every struggle in your life has shaped you into the person you are today. Be thankful for the hard times, they can only make you stronger."*

This story was created from publicly available information. It does not suggest endorsement of Hopeful Minds, or any affiliation by known celebrity to our program. All information is for illustrative purposes for youth, to demonstrate skills used to create, maintain, and grow hope.

LESSON TAKEAWAY (GROUP DISCUSSION):

☀ *Take turns planning times in the upcoming week when you can engage in a Happiness Habit each day.*

☀ *What is one piece of information you found most helpful in this lesson?*

☀ *How will you incorporate the information you learned in this lesson to your life this week?*

☀️ *Keanu Reeves practiced numerous Happiness Habits to help manage the heavy events in his life. How could regular practice of the Happiness Habits impact Keanu's general mood?*

Go back to the very first worksheet on page 11, where you identified your hope hero. Fill in the Happiness Habits your hope hero uses to help maintain positive feelings.

WEEKLY HOPE ACTIVATION

Inspired Actions for Hope are the things you can do to reinforce these lessons and begin to bring hope skills into your daily life. Choose at least one of the actions below to complete before moving on from this lesson.

☀️ Create a giant sunflower. Put a sunflower center up on your wall and print one to three sunflower petals. Write at least one happiness habit on each petal.

☀️ Take time to practice at least one new Happiness Habit each day this week. What Happiness Habits will you practice this week and when will you plan to practice it? Who will help hold you accountable for practicing the Happiness Habits?

1. _____   5. _____

2. _____   6. _____

3. _____   7. _____

4. _____

Think of one Happiness Habit you practiced this week and answer the following questions:

How did your body feel before practicing your Happiness Habit?

How did your body feel during your Happiness Habit?

How did your body feel after practicing your Happiness Habit?

☀ Mindfulness Activity

Mindfulness, or presence, is the act of focusing your awareness on the present moment. It seems like a simple concept, but being fully present is actually a lot harder than it sounds. In fact, most of us are only present about 50% of the time. That means that the other 50% of the time, we are so busy focusing on other things. You might be worrying about the future, ruminating on the past, or just scrolling through reels on your phone.

Mindfulness is important for staying in your upstairs brain. Scientific research has found that the less time you spend in the present moment, the more stress you feel, and the less happy you are. Mindfulness matters.

However, being mindful is difficult, so it's okay if you struggle at first. It means not looking at our phones or tablets. It means not worrying about the future or thinking about what happened in the past. Presence also means not multitasking when we are doing things.

Mindful meditation allows you to take charge of your brain so you have even more control when you experience negative emotions. Mindfulness meditation helps slow down your mind so that when you are triggered, you learn to pause.

Mindfulness Exercise #1: Check out this exercise that involves mindfully listening to music. *(Page 196)*

Mindfulness Exercise #2: Try the following breathing mindfulness meditation for three minutes *(Page 196)*

NOTES

Post your completed activities on social media using the following hashtags to help us teach the lessons. Make sure to tag us @ifredorg and @theshinehopecompany.

#HopefulMindsTeens #Hope #ShineHope #ScienceofHope
#HappinessHabits #HappyHormones #Mindfulness

APPINESS HABITS

Happiness Habits are healthy, long-term actions that cause your brain to release happiness hormones including endorphins, dopamine, serotonin, and oxytocin. Happiness Habits help you stay in your upstairs brain, where you access the problem-solving skills, collaboration, and passion critical for hope.

Positive Feelings

Positive feelings, the first ingredient of hope, are feelings that are located in your upstairs brain like wonder, joy, and peace that make it easier to overcome obstacles that get in the way of hope. You proactively manage the emotional despair of hopelessness using Stress Skills and use your Happiness Habits to stay in your upstairs brain, where you then energetically move towards your goals in life.

Activating purpose	Exercising / Nutrition	Volunteering
Pursuing passion	Creating / listening to music	Wonder/Awe
Utilizing strengths	Dancing / Singing	Quality sleep
Meditation	Drawing / Painting	Doodling
Smiling	Gratitude	

Module 6:

The Second Key to Shine Hope: Happiness Habits Part 2

Module 6: The Second Key to Shine Hope: Happiness Habits Part 2

The last module helped you identify your Happiness Habits; this module helps you tap into the second part of Happiness Habits, which involves using the Happiness Habits to help you identify your strengths and passions in life. Figuring out your purpose, or your "why" in life can help you develop goals (i.e., Inspired Actions) and then take the steps to meet those goals.

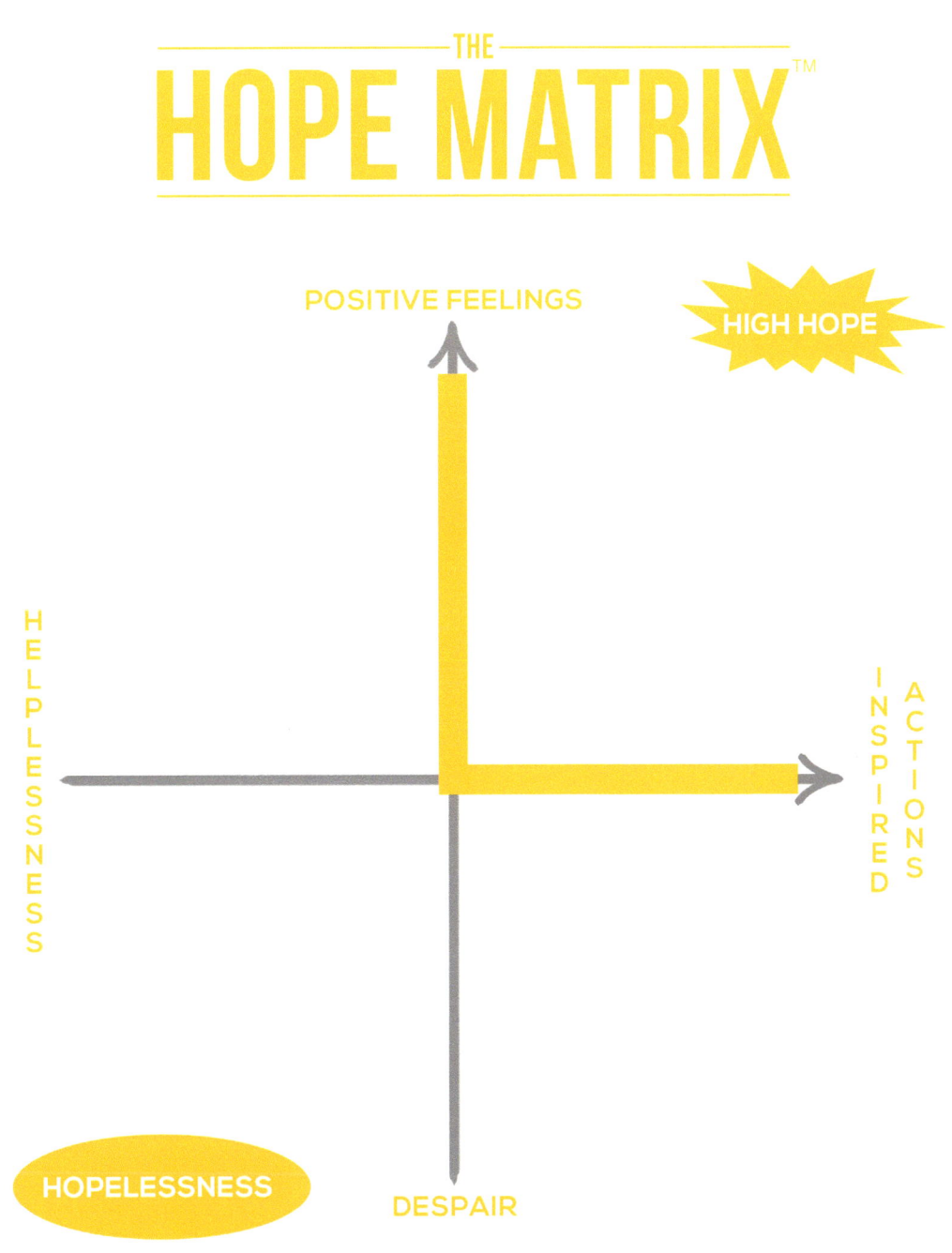

There are 8 billion people on the planet. With that many people, it can sometimes feel like we don't matter or we aren't important. However, nothing could be further from the truth. You are important. Each and every person brings a unique value to the world that no other person can bring. No matter what anyone tells you, it's true. **You matter.**

We all have equal value on this earth and a special purpose here. Your mission is to find what your purpose is and enjoy the journey while you pursue it. Pursuing your purpose can drastically increase your hope. In fact, the second ingredient for hope, inspired actions, is dedicated to pursuing goals that help you fulfill your purpose.

But how do you find your purpose? You can discover your purpose by identifying your strengths and your passions.

STRENGTHS

In Lesson 1, you took the VIA Character Strengths Finder to identify your strengths.

What were your five main strengths?

1
2
3
4
5

PASSION

Discovering your passions is incredibly important for your personal happiness and success. When you find activities and interests that genuinely excite you, it brings a deep sense of fulfillment and purpose to your life. Pursuing your passions motivates you to work hard, overcome challenges, and become the best version of yourself.

It also helps you understand who you are, develop important skills, and make confident choices about your future career. Exploring different passions expands your horizons, makes you well-rounded, and opens doors to exciting opportunities. So, don't be afraid to explore and follow what truly lights up your heart – it can lead you to a truly rewarding and meaningful life journey.

Our emotions are like powerful clues that help us discover our passions. When we feel really strong emotions, like excitement, happiness, or even sadness, anger, or fear, it's a sign that something truly matters to us. Emotions work like a compass, pointing us in the direction of activities and pursuits that make us feel fulfilled and happy.

Sometimes the source of our greatest pain can be a source of our passion. For example, if someone has experienced a lot of teasing, they may feel passionate about equity or kindness. Someone who has lost a loved one to gun violence may feel passionate about safety and peace, we must use our feelings to guide us into what we should put our time and energy into.

By paying attention to our emotions, we can uncover our true passions and live a more meaningful and purposeful life.

 ## GROUP ACTIVITY

☀ *Reflect on Personal Experiences: Think about and talk through times when you experienced strong emotions, such as joy or pain related to an experience. These experiences can be related to hobbies, personal experiences, school, or anything in your life that has caused a strong emotional reaction.*

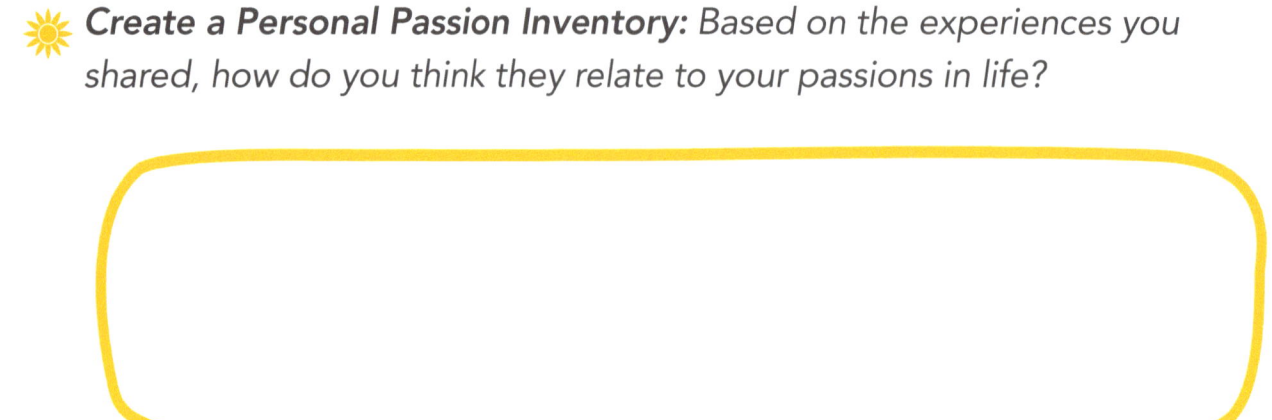

☀ **Create a Personal Passion Inventory:** *Based on the experiences you shared, how do you think they relate to your passions in life?*

☀ **Connect Passion and Strength:** *Discuss connections between your strengths and passions. Think about how your strengths have contributed to the success or enjoyment of your passions. For example, if one of your strengths is leadership, how might leadership have contributed to your sense of fulfillment when engaging in a passion?*

PURPOSE

One's purpose in life can be found in the simple act of being present and letting go of expectations. Embracing the present moment allows us to fully engage with the world around us, savoring each experience and finding joy in the little things. By releasing expectations, we free ourselves from the burden of rigid plans and outcomes, allowing life to unfold naturally.

Instead of striving for specific outcomes, we can focus on growth, learning, and being open to new opportunities. Living without expectations grants us the freedom to explore our passions, connect with others on a deeper level, and embrace the beauty of life's unpredictable journey. In being present and open, we discover a sense of purpose that is grounded in authenticity, contentment, and the genuine pursuit of happiness.

GROUP ACTIVITY

Create a purposeful vision board!

Gather materials like a poster board, magazines, scissors, glue, and markers. Start by identifying a specific area of growth you'd like to focus on in the future. It could be something you deeply care about, such as promoting environmental awareness or supporting a social cause.

Search for visuals that represent your purpose, whether it's pictures, words, or quotes, and cut them out or create your own drawings. Arrange these visuals on your vision board in a visually appealing way and secure them with glue or tape.

For instance, if your purpose is to organize a community recycling campaign, set a goal like collecting 1,000 pounds of recyclable materials by the end of the school year. Display your vision board in a place where you'll see it every day to remind yourself of your purpose and the goal you've set.

Take action towards your goal by breaking it down into smaller steps and consistently working on them. Remember, your vision board and goal are unique to you, and you can update them as your passions and aspirations evolve. Let your vision board inspire and motivate you as you work towards making a meaningful impact.

PURPOSE AND HOPE:
TYING EVERYTHING TOGETHER

Purpose and hope go hand in hand, especially for teenagers. Purpose gives you a clear direction and meaning in life, while hope keeps you optimistic about the future. When you have a purpose, you know what you're striving for, and it gives you hope that you can achieve your goals and make a positive impact.

Purpose helps you overcome challenges and stay resilient, while hope fuels your belief in positive change. Together, purpose and hope provide a sense of meaning, fulfillment, and a bright outlook on what lies ahead. So, discover your purpose, hold onto hope, and believe in the incredible possibilities that await you.

HOPE HERO SPOTLIGHT

KEN JEONG

Ken Jeong is an American-Korean comedian and actor who is known for his outrageous acting. Ken wasn't always an actor.

When he was in school, Ken knew that his purpose was making people feel better, so he decided that he wanted to be a doctor. However, after performing in a comedy skit at school, Ken realized he also had a passion for making people laugh, and humor was also a Happiness Habit Ken practiced.

Ken had two passions that could help him achieve his purpose, and he wanted to pursue both of them. So, during the day, he worked as a doctor, and during the evening, he performed stand-up comedy.

Today, Ken Jeong is still pursuing his passion for making people feel better. He still works full-time as an actor and comedian. And, during the coronavirus pandemic, he used his medical background to help people understand the science and medical terms associated with the corona virus.

Ken is proof that Happiness Habits and passions can go hand in hand. He used his Happiness Habit of humor to identify and pursue his passion of becoming a comedian. As long as you use your Happiness Habits to help maintain positive feelings, and listen to your feelings, you have the potential to identify and pursue your passion.*

This story was created from publicly available information. It does not suggest endorsement of Hopeful Minds, or any affiliation by known celebrity to our program. All information is for illustrative purposes for youth, to demonstrate skills used to create, maintain, and grow hope.

LESSON TAKEAWAY (GROUP DISCUSSION):

☀ *How do your emotions relate to your passions? How do your passions relate to your purpose?*

☀ *What is one piece of information you found most helpful in this lesson?*

☀ *How will you incorporate the information you learned in this lesson to your life this week?*

☀ *Ken Jeong gives us an example of someone who pursued their passion as a career option. With permission, search for the Stress Skills Ken used while pursuing his passions.*

WEEKLY HOPE ACTIVATION

Inspired Actions for Hope are the things you can do to reinforce these lessons and begin to bring hope skills into your daily life. Choose at least one of the actions below to complete before moving to the next lesson.

☀ Start exploring your passions further. Engage in different activities, join clubs or organizations related to your interests, or seek out opportunities to learn more about those subjects. Try new experiences, even if they seem outside your comfort zone. Pay attention to how each activity makes you feel and whether it truly sparks your passion.

☀ Search for careers that align with your purpose.

☀ Pay attention to how your emotions relate to your passions throughout the week. How might they inform your purpose?

Post your completed activities on social media using the following hashtags to help us teach the lessons. Make sure to tag us **@ifredorg** and **@theshinehopecompany.**

#HopefulMindsTeens #Hope #ShineHope #My Strengths (and share them on social) #Passion #Purpose

Module 7:
The Third Key to Shine Hope: Inspired Actions

Module 7: The Third Key to Shine Hope: Inspired Actions

Inspired Actions, the "I" in Shine, are the goal-setting skills that help you set and reach your goals. They are what help you move from motivational helplessness to Inspired Actions on the Hope Matrix.

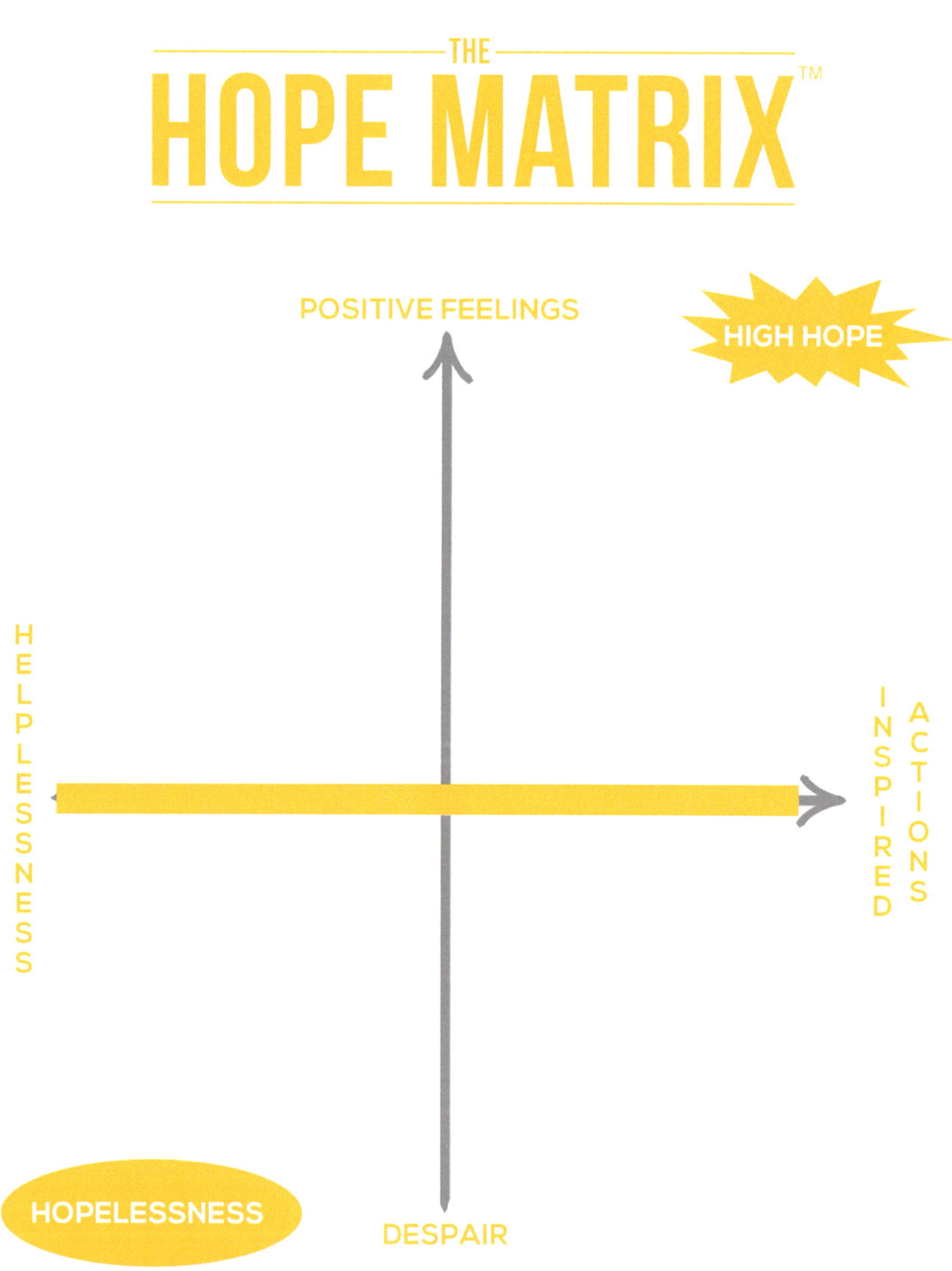

Once you've started understanding your passion and purpose, the next step is to set your goals. Keep in mind that pursuing goals is also considered a Happiness Habit. Even if you don't reach your goals, the simple act of setting the goal and working towards it can help you maintain a hopeful outlook.

Goals are like targets that individuals set for themselves to achieve in different aspects of their lives, such as self-improvement, career, relationships, and health. They are specific and measurable objectives that we work towards within a certain time frame.

Now, let's relate goals to hope. Remember that hope is all about positive feelings and inspired actions. When we have hope, we believe in the possibility of good things happening and imagine a better future. Inspired actions are the goals we set for ourselves that come from our inner passion and enthusiasm.

Hope fuels our motivation and optimism to pursue these goals. It's like the emotional drive that pushes us forward, giving us the courage to work hard and stay focused on achieving our dreams. So, when we have hope, we are more likely to set meaningful goals and take inspired actions to make them come true.

To help ensure you are setting goals focused on hope, we encourage you to use the goal-setting techniques outlined in the next two parts. They include:

☀️ Achievement Goals   ☀️ SMART Goals

☀️ Intrinsic Goals   ☀️ Stretch Goals

☀️ The WOOP Framework   ☀️ Micro-Goals and the Stepping Method

Once you learn more about each of these frameworks and goals, you will practice using all six to brainstorm and set goals that move you toward hope.

ACHIEVEMENT VS. AVOIDANCE GOALS

When you are setting goals, you want to be setting achievement goals, not avoidance goals. Achievement goals are goals that focus on self-improvement and progress. Avoidance goals are goals that you set to avoid an outcome, such as a mistake or a failure.

Research shows that when you set achievement goals you are more likely to reach the goals you set. Achievement goals are associated with positive achievement outcomes, such as high levels of effort, interest in the task, and the use of deep learning strategies. These types of goals also help you stay in your upstairs brain and cultivate hope.

 **GROUP ACTIVITY**

For the goals below, identify whether they are achievement or avoidance goals. If they are avoidance goals, rewrite them as achievement goals.

I want to pass my math test to feel good about myself.

I want to pass my math test so that I don't get grounded.

I want to practice free throws so I play my best.

I want to practice free throws so that I don't miss during the game.

I want to take 20 minutes each day to meditate to improve my mental health.

GROUP DISCUSSION

☀ Do you typically set achievement or avoidance goals? If you typically set avoidance goals, why do you think that they seem easier to set?

☀ How can you start setting achievement goals?

SELF-REFLECTION

What is an achievement goal you'd like to meet?

INTRINSIC GOALS VS. EXTRINSIC GOALS

It is also important to set intrinsic goals, rather than extrinsic goals. Extrinsic goals pertain to external achievements, such as wealth, power, or fame. Intrinsic goals, on the other hand, are goals that pertain to your passions and core values. You'll know you are setting an intrinsic goal if it is focused on one of three things: meaningful relationships, personal growth, or community contributions.

GROUP ACTIVITY

Look at the goals below. Are the achievement goals intrinsic goals or extrinsic goals?

I want to pass my math test so that I don't get grounded.	*Intrinsic Goals Extrinsic Goals*
I want to practice free throws so that I can make every shot next game.	*Intrinsic Goals Extrinsic Goals*
I want to practice free throws so that I don't miss during the game.	*Intrinsic Goals Extrinsic Goals*
I want to take 20 minutes each day to meditate to improve my mental health.	*Intrinsic Goals Extrinsic Goals*

 # GROUP DISCUSSION

☀ Research shows that extrinsic goals lead to higher rates of anxiety and depression, while intrinsic goals are associated with happiness and hope. Why do you think that is?

☀ Do you set goals? Why is goal-setting important to you? How does goal-setting relate to hope? Why might it be important to write down your goals?

WOOP

When brainstorming your goals, you can use the WOOP method.

The WOOP method includes four steps: W(wish), O(outcome), O(obstacle), and P(plan):

WISH
Think about your purpose. What is the most important wish or concern related to your purpose? Pick a wish that is challenging but that you can still fulfill.

OUTCOME
What would be the best possible outcome if your wish came true? How would fulfilling your wish make you feel?

OBSTACLE
What is within you or in your environment that keeps you from fulfilling your wish?

PLAN
Identify one action you can take or one thought you can think to overcome your obstacle. Then, make an if-then plan: IF (I encounter this obstacle) THEN (I will use this solution).

Use the WOOP Method to brainstorm one goal for your school, relationships, health, community, or this program.

WISH

OUTCOME

OBSTACLE

PLAN

 **GROUP ACTIVITY**

Share your wishes and help each other brainstorm outcomes, obstacles, and plans.

SMART GOALS

When setting goals, you want to ensure that you set a number of SMART goals Goals that are Specific, Measurable, Attainable, Relevant, and Time-bound. Let's talk about each of these individually:

 ### SPECIFIC
Be specific about your goal. Think about these questions when creating your goal: What needs to be accomplished? Who is responsible for it? What steps will you take to achieve it?

 ### MEASURABLE
Can you measure your progress? If this goal will take a long time to achieve, set shorter-term goals to reach along the way.

 ### ACHIEVABLE
Are you inspired and motivated to reach your goal? Do you have the tools or skills you need? If not, do you know how you can get them?

 ### RELEVANT
Does your goal make sense? Does it go along with what you are trying to achieve in the bigger picture?

 ### TIME-BOUND
Is your timing realistic? Can you achieve your goal in the time period set? Think about what you may want to achieve at the halfway point.

Look at the goal you set above (The WISH in your WOOP Framework). Write and check if it meets the SMART criteria. If it doesn't, brainstorm ways you can change it to make it SMART.

GOAL:

Is it:

◯ **S**PECIFIC?

◯ **M**EASURABLE?

◯ **A**CHIEVABLE?

◯ **R**ELEVANT?

◯ **T**IME-BOUND?

◯ Is it an achievement goal?

◯ Is it an intrinsic goal?

 **GROUP DISCUSSION**

☀ *What was the most challenging part of setting your SMART Goal? Why?*

☀ *How can you overcome that challenge?*

STRETCH GOALS

Stretch goals are long-term goals that you set to reach your purpose; they should stretch and challenge you, and inspire you to keep moving forward toward the future. Your stretch goals may be things like "make it to the state competition" or "go to a top university."

What is one stretch goal you have for your life?

GROUP DISCUSSION

☀ *What is the difference between stretch goals and SMART goals?*

☀ *Why is it important to have both SMART goals and stretch goals?*

YOUR GOALS AND HOPE:
TYING EVERYTHING TOGETHER

The most important thing to remember about goals is that they should always be set from your upstairs brain. If you are in your downstairs brain, your first goal should be getting back into your upstairs brain so you can use your inspired actions.

One of the causes of hopelessness is setting an unrealistic goal or having set your goal from a place of negativity. When you set goals that are confusing, broad, unspecific, stemming from anger or fear, or impractical, you are setting yourself up for failure.

Instead, you should be setting goals that will encourage you to continue moving forward with positive feelings and inspired actions.

When you are setting goals, remember that you are more than just your classes or your future career. It's important to set goals not just in your professional life, but also in the other areas of your life that are important to you. In our course, we cover the following areas:

☀ School

☀ Relationships or Personal Life

☀ Health and Well-being

☀ Hope

☀ Community

Each one of us defines "success" in these areas of our lives differently. We also prioritize the areas of our lives differently from one another. That's okay. You can find success, meaning, happiness, and hope in any of these areas. Once you have identified what success in these areas means to you, it can be easier to think about your strengths, passions, and purpose in life.

GROUP ACTIVITY

Setting goals for each area of your life can help you maintain a healthy balance. In the space below, create a vision board for goals in three areas of your life (i.e., school, relationships, health, community, work, etc) using images, drawings, magazine clippings, or whatever else you can find!

GROUP DISCUSSION

☀ *What areas of your life do you set more goals around (e.g., school, social relationships, future, etc.)? How do you think prioritizing these areas impacts your hope levels?*

☀ *What areas in your life would it be beneficial to set more goals around?*

VISION BOARD

HOPE HERO SPOTLIGHT

SERENA WILLIAMS

Serena Williams is a famous professional tennis player who is often called one of the Greatest Tennis Players of All Time. She has won 23 major single titles, 39 Grand Slam titles, and four Olympic gold medals.

Serena Williams discovered her Happiness Habit of playing tennis was something she was passionate about when she started tennis lessons at three years old. Serena was instantly passionate about the competition and mental challenges of tennis. Serena decided that she wanted to fulfill her purpose by being a professional tennis player, and she set SMART goals for her tennis skills improvement and the number of practice sessions each week.

Over the next five years, she won 46 of the 49 tournaments she entered. Serena continued to excel in tennis until, at the age of 16, she accomplished her stretch goal and became a professional tennis player.

Once Serena Williams became a professional tennis player, she set a new SMART goal for herself. Serena decided that she wanted to win more major tournaments than any other female tennis player in history. Serena understands the power of SMART goals, and she uses them to make herself the best athlete she can be. Like Serena, you have the ability to use your positive mindset and inspired actions to set your own SMART goals and achieve your dreams.*

This story was created from publicly available information. It does not suggest endorsement of Hopeful Minds, or any affiliation by known celebrity to our program. All information is for illustrative purposes for youth, to demonstrate skills used to create, maintain, and grow hope.

☀ *What is one piece of information you found most helpful in this lesson?*

☀ *How will you incorporate the information you learned in this lesson to your life this week?*

☀ *Serena Williams set goals surrounding tennis to help her improve and become a professional tennis player. With parent permission, search for more information on Serena's goal to pinpoint how it was a SMART goal.*

Go back to the very first worksheet on page 11, where you identified your hope hero. Fill in the inspired actions of your hope hero.

WEEKLY HOPE ACTIVATION

Inspired Actions for Hope are the things you can do to reinforce these lessons and begin to bring hope skills into your daily life. Choose at least one of the actions below to complete before moving to the next lesson.

☀ Set a goal for yourself that you can achieve in the next week using the worksheets provided.

☀ Check in with your group mates at least once in the following days to see where they are in meeting their goal.

I want to pass my math test to feel good about myself.

Achievement

I want to pass my math test so that I don't get grounded.

Avoidance

I want to practice free throws so I play my best.

Achievement

I want to practice free throws so that I don't miss during the game.

Avoidance

I want to take 20 minutes each day to meditate to improve my mental health.

Achievement

I want to pass my math test so that I don't get grounded.

Intrinsic Goals   *Extrinsic Goals*

I want to practice free throws so that I can make every shot next game.

Intrinsic Goals   *Extrinsic Goals*

I want to practice free throws so that I don't miss during the game.

Intrinsic Goals   *Extrinsic Goals*

I want to take 20 minutes each day to meditate to improve my mental health.

Intrinsic Goals   *Extrinsic Goals*

Post your completed activities on social media using the following hashtags to help us teach the lessons. Make sure to tag us **@ifredorg** and **@theshinehopecompany**

#HopefulMinds #Teens #Hope #ShineHope #ScienceofHope #InspiredActions #Goals #SMARTGoals #WOOP #IGotGoals

INSPIRED ACTIONS

Inspired Actions, the second ingredient of hope, are the deliberate steps you take toward your goals in life. Inspired Actions help you to move away from the motivational helplessness, the second ingredient of hopelessness, and toward what you are hopeful for in life.

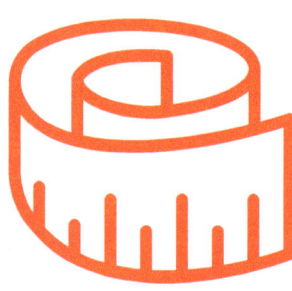

Types of Goals:

WOOP   SMART

Achievement   Stretch

Intrinsic   Micro-Goals

Pathways, Agency, and Regoaling

Obstacles are inevitable, and sometimes you can't reach the goal as you intended. It is important to embrace obstacles to goals, learn to pivot or reevaluate, be flexible and adaptable, and never be afraid to ask for help.

If a goal seems too big, use the stepping process or create micro-goals to chunk it down into smaller goals. Think of one thing you can do in the next 20 minutes. And know when you need to re-goal.

Module 8:
The Third Key to Shine Hope: Inspired Actions
Part 2

Module 8: The Third Key to Shine Hope: Inspired Actions Part 2

In the previous module, you acquired the skills related to Inspired Actions. In this module, we'll delve into the next aspect of Inspired Actions, which centers around devising strategies to effectively navigate challenges that may arise as you strive to achieve your goals. While obstacles are a natural part of any goal pursuit, proactively identifying strategies to overcome them from the outset can significantly contribute to keeping you on track towards successfully attaining your goals.

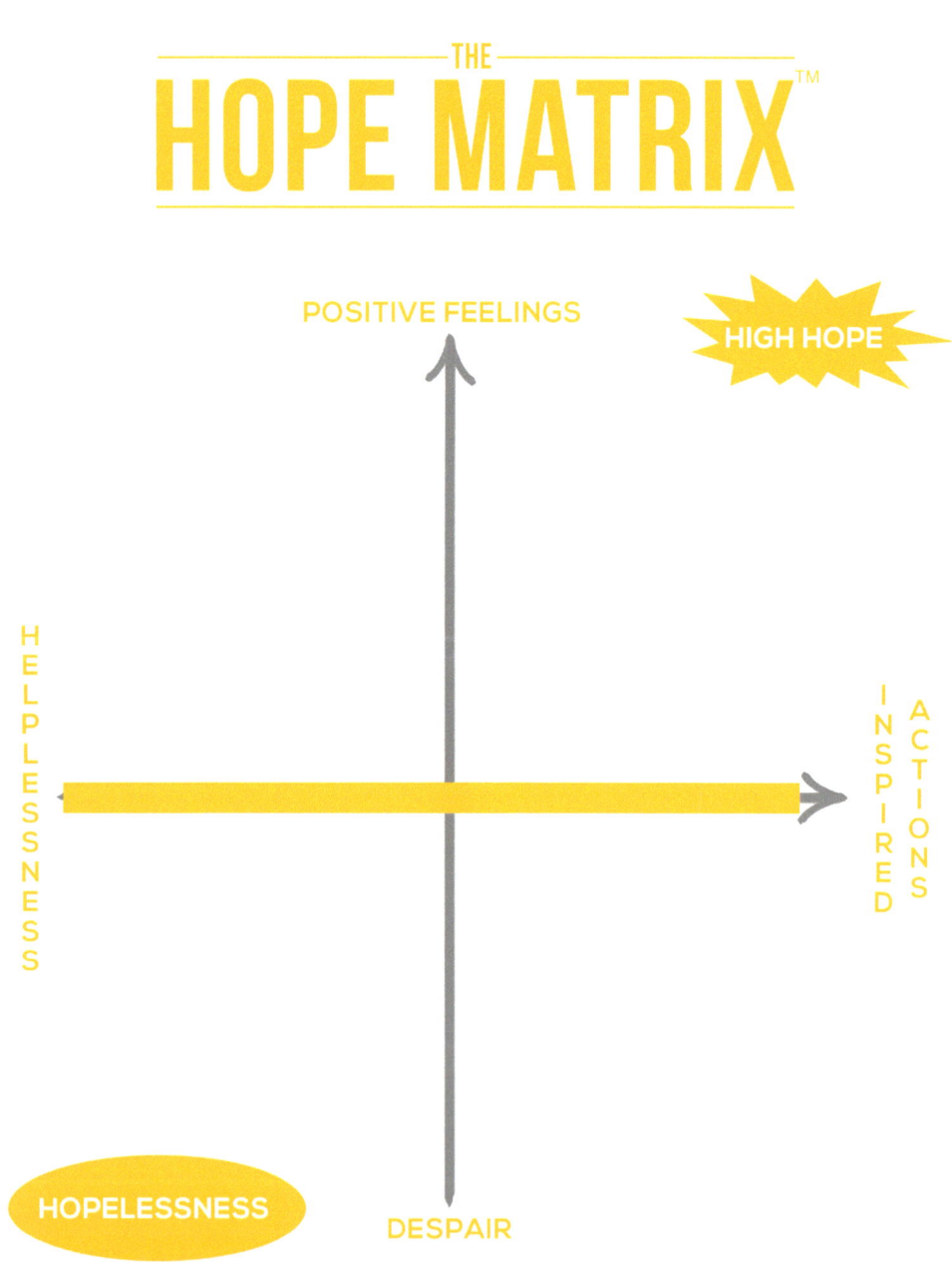

THE INEVITABILITY OF OBSTACLES

Once you've set your goals and begun chasing after them, you might come across some challenges along the way. Life is full of obstacles, and it's important to be prepared for them and handle them with the right attitude. How you deal with obstacles emotionally and the strategies you use to overcome them can greatly impact your long-term success. Our goal is to provide you with the necessary tools to conquer the inevitable hurdles that will come your way as you work towards your goals.

Working towards goals is equivalent to completing a maze puzzle. With enough problem-solving and redirection, you will eventually get to the end of the puzzle or meet your goal.

In general, people react one of four ways when they encounter an obstacle:

We see the obstacle as a puzzle to solve.

We see the obstacle as an opportunity to grow.

We see the obstacle as a threat.

We see the obstacle as an indication that we cannot succeed, or that we are a failure.

When you react with options 1 or 2, you are able to use positive feelings and inspired actions to successfully navigate the obstacle in a healthy way. When you react with options 3 and 4, you are setting yourself up for failure and hopelessness.

When you see your obstacles as a threat, you are much more likely to let them keep you from reaching your goals. However, every path will have obstacles. Therefore, if you want to be hopeful and continue moving forward, you have to learn how to face them head-on.

Despair and helplessness as we meet obstacles are normal; it is how we manage them that counts.

 **GROUP ACTIVITY**

Read the following vignette and discuss how Carlos could have used hope skills to overcome the obstacle.

In the bustling heart of the city lived Carlos, a determined and resilient young man with a dream. His goal was to secure a scholarship to attend a prestigious college and break the cycle of limited opportunities in his community. He knew education was his ticket to a brighter future.

However, Carlos faced significant obstacles on his path to success. He attended a school with limited resources, where overcrowded classrooms made it challenging to receive individual attention. The outdated textbooks and lack of extracurricular activities stifled his thirst for knowledge. Yet, Carlos refused to be deterred.

Outside the classroom, the streets of his neighborhood presented another set of challenges. Gangs and crime were a constant presence, and peer pressure to engage in negative activities loomed over him. Carlos had to navigate carefully to avoid falling into the clutches of a dangerous lifestyle.

GROUP DISCUSSION

☀ *What obstacles was Carlos trying to overcome? How could he use hope skills to overcome the obstacles?*

☀ *What about Carlos' story can you relate to?*

☀ *Recognize 1-2 moments in your life where you have hit an obstacle (either current or something you think you dealt with poorly). As a group, talk through how one could use hope skills to navigate the obstacle. Then, talk through how your strengths and values can help you overcome obstacles.*

STEPS FOR OVERCOMING OBSTACLES

When you set your next goal, try to overcome obstacles using these steps:

1. Prepare for Potential Obstacles: When you set goals, you should also think critically about the obstacles you may encounter. As you work through your goal worksheets, also take time to write down what obstacles you may face and what you can do to either prevent or manage the obstacle. By visualizing your obstacles ahead of time, you increase your ability to overcome them when they arise. By visualizing your obstacles ahead of time, you increase your ability to overcome them when they arise, even if it isn't the same obstacle. Consider downloading our no cost goal meditation. *(Page 196)*

2. Reframe the Obstacles: Sometimes when we are faced with an obstacle, it can feel nearly impossible to work through it, especially if it is negatively framed. One way of helping our brains stretch beyond the negativity is to re-frame the problem we are solving. For example, instead of How can we strengthen this team's weakness, we can re-frame the obstacle as How can we capitalize on the team's strengths?

3. Accept the Obstacles: No one wants to encounter obstacles. However, no matter how much planning you do in Step 1, obstacles are still inevitable. It is, therefore, important that you accept their place in your journey. When you learn to enjoy the journey, it makes it easier to accept the challenges. Accepting the obstacles you face will also make it easier to investigate them with your upstairs brain.

4. Acknowledge Your Feelings: When you face an obstacle, you may feel any number of emotions, such as disappointment, stress, anger, or hopelessness. It's important that you let yourself feel these emotions and listen to what they are teaching you. However, once you have identified the emotions you are feeling, you need to use Stress Skills to release the energy associated with them. If you try to overcome an obstacle when in your downstairs brain, you are much less likely to think of a successful solution.

5. Approach the Obstacles with Your Upstairs Brain: Using inspired actions and problem-solving skills, start to look for a solution using your upstairs brain. Remember, your upstairs brain is where your critical thinking, creativity, logic, and hope are located.

Use the steps above to prepare for obstacles associated with the goals you set in Module 7.

Write down each of the goals you set for yourself in the last lesson and brainstorm potential obstacles and solutions.

Remember, planning for obstacles ahead of time increases your ability to effectively manage them when they come your way.

SMART GOAL:

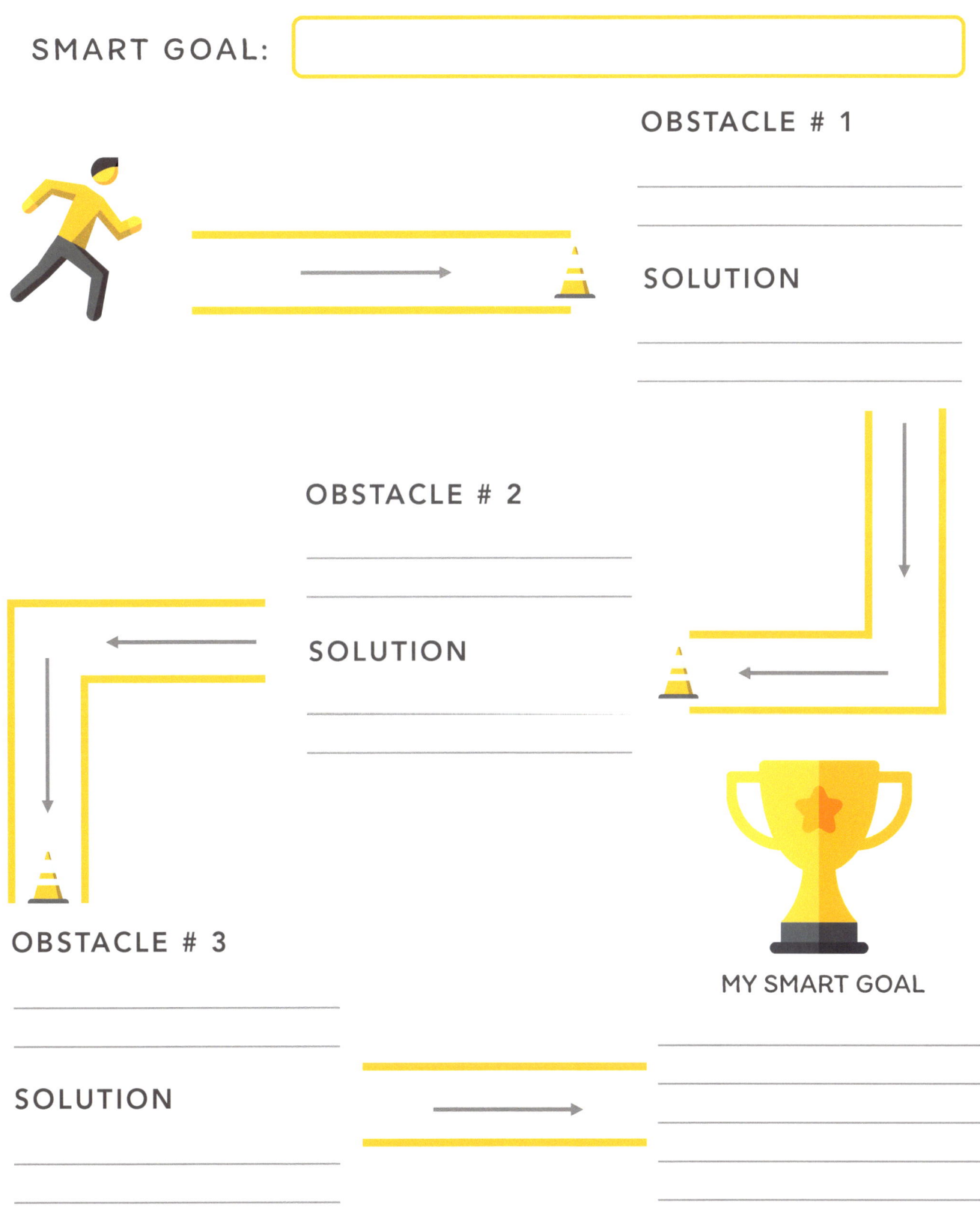

OBSTACLE # 1

_____

_____

SOLUTION

_____

_____

OBSTACLE # 2

_____

_____

SOLUTION

_____

_____

OBSTACLE # 3

_____

_____

SOLUTION

_____

_____

MY SMART GOAL

_____

_____

_____

_____

☀ *Help each other brainstorm solutions to the obstacles you identified. Was the group able to come up with additional solutions you hadn't previously considered?*

Sometimes, even when you do your best to think of a solution, the obstacle can still feel unbeatable. When that is the case, we have a few tools that you can use to try to find a solution:

1. Ask For Help When You Need It: Asking for ideas from others can be very helpful when overcoming obstacles. Other people are likely to know resources and have skills that you don't have.

2. Break it Down: Sometimes obstacles feel overwhelming because they seem too large to manage. Break the obstacle down into smaller pieces that you can overcome one step at a time using micro goals.

Micro-goals are the small, achievable goals that help you move toward your stretch goals. They are the steps in the stepping process that help you continue looking towards the future. For example, if your stretch goal is to run a marathon, your short-term goals may be "running three miles per day" or "registering for next year's marathon." Your medium-range goal may be "running a half marathon by January."

On its own, each moderate goal seems accomplishable, and they help you stay in your upstairs brain as you move towards your stretch goal.

Think back to your stretch goal from the last lesson. What are ten micro-goals you can set to help you reach your stretch goal?

1. _____   6. _____

2. _____   7. _____

3. _____   8. _____

4. _____   9. _____

5. _____   10. _____

3. Reevaluate: Don't be afraid to reevaluate the path you take to reach your goal. Sometimes, the best way to overcome an obstacle is to sidestep it. Once you overcome the obstacle or find a way around it, make sure you re-examine the steps you need to take to reach your goal.

One important thing about this process is that encountering insurmountable obstacles does not equal failing to reach a goal. Instead, they are learning opportunities. When we step back and re-evaluate our path to a goal, we have more knowledge than we had before and are more capable of finding a way forward.

This is just like solving the maze at the beginning of this lesson. You may have taken a wrong turn at the start and had to go back. This wasn't a waste of time, it was learning. Now you KNOW that turning left isn't going to get you to the goal, and you need to turn right instead.

4. Regoal! Sometimes, once you try all of your methods for overcoming obstacles, an obstacle is still insurmountable. When you cannot overcome an obstacle, it is important to reevaluate and regoal, which allows you to keep moving forward. For example, if someone breaks their leg and can no longer become an athlete, they can fall back on their other strengths and passions to set a new goal.

5. Celebrate! The journey is important, but so is the destination. Make sure that you take time to celebrate your accomplishments.

Choose one of the goals above and answer the following questions:

Goal: _____

Obstacle you might face: _____

Ask for help. Who are people that can help you overcome this obstacle?

_____

Break it down. What is the first step you can take to overcome
the obstacle?

_____

Reevaluate. Brainstorm ways you can change your goal to sidestep this
obstacle and still achieve your purpose.

_____

Celebrate. How will accomplishing this goal make you feel?

_____

Regoal. What is an alternative goal you might have if the initial goal cannot
be achieved?

_____

 **GROUP DISCUSSION**

☀ How could you manage the emotional despair and helplessness that may
arise when faced with regoaling? What skills can you use?

OVERCOMING OBSTACLES AND HOPE: TYING EVERYTHING TOGETHER

Overcoming obstacles is closely intertwined with hope. As a teenager, you may face various challenges and setbacks on your path toward achieving your goals and dreams. It is during these times of struggle that hope becomes your guiding light.

Hope fuels your determination and resilience, enabling you to push past obstacles with the belief that a better outcome awaits you. It provides the strength to persevere, the courage to take risks, and the optimism that things will eventually improve. Embracing hope empowers you to view obstacles as temporary roadblocks rather than permanent barriers, and it reminds you that with perseverance and a positive mindset, you can overcome any challenge that comes your way.

Remember, no matter how tough things may seem, hope can inspire you to keep moving forward and ultimately achieve the success and fulfillment you desire.

HOPE HERO SPOTLIGHT

JANE GOODALL

In the heart of Africa, a determined young woman named Jane Goodall embarked on an incredible journey. Her goal was to study chimpanzees in their natural habitat, but the challenges she faced were as wild as the jungle itself.

Jane's first challenge was gaining the trust of the chimpanzees. Day after day, she sat quietly, patiently observing from a distance. But the chimpanzees remained wary of her presence. Undeterred, Jane realized that to achieve her original goal of close observation, she had to set a different goal – to earn their trust. So, she started by offering them small gifts of bananas and gaining ground one step at a time.

As weeks turned into months, Jane's determination paid off. The chimpanzees began to accept her as part of their environment. With their trust, Jane could now study their behaviors up close, unlocking secrets of their world.

Jane's journey teaches us that sometimes, challenges require us to adapt and shift our goals. By being flexible and persistent, we can overcome obstacles and find success in unexpected ways. Just as Jane transformed her initial setbacks into triumphs, we too can transform challenges into opportunities on the path to achieving our dreams.*

This story was created from publicly available information. It does not suggest endorsement of Hopeful Minds, or any affiliation by known celebrity to our program. All information is for illustrative purposes for youth, to demonstrate skills used to create, maintain, and grow hope.

LESSON TAKEAWAY (GROUP DISCUSSION):

☀ *What is one piece of information you found most helpful in this lesson?*

☀ *How will you incorporate the information you learned in this lesson to your life this week?*

☀ *Jane Goodall faced challenges while trying to reach her goal of observing chimpanzees. How did Jane practice regoaling to better observe the behavior of chimpanzees?*

Go back to the very first worksheet on page 11, where you identified your hope hero. Add more information next to "I" about how your hope hero overcame obstacles while working towards their goal.

Go back to the very first worksheet on page 11, where you identified your hope hero. Add more information next to "I" about how your hope hero overcame obstacles while working towards their goal.

WEEKLY HOPE ACTIVATION

Inspired Actions for Hope are the things you can do to reinforce these lessons and begin to bring hope skills into your daily life. Choose at least one of the actions below to complete before moving to the next lesson.

☀ Using a posterboard or a portion of the whiteboard, brainstorm obstacles you may face as a group this year and how you can overcome them. Keep the list up where you can see it so that, as you face challenges, you can refer to the list for helpful solutions.

☀ Pull out the giant sunflower you created from part five. Print out 1-3 sunflower petals and write out potential obstacles you may face throughout the year and at least one solution you can use to overcome them.

NOTES

Post your completed activities on social media using the following hashtags to help us teach the lessons. Make sure to tag us **@ifredorg** and **@theshinehopecompany**

#HopefulMindsTeens #Hope #ShineHope #ScienceofHope #OvercomingObstacles

Module 9:
The Fourth Key to Shine Hope: Shi**n**e Hope: **N**ourishing Networks

Module 9: The Fourth Key to Shine Hope: Nourishing Networks

The fourth Key to Shine Hope is Nourishing Networks, also known as your social support. Building and maintaining a Nourishing Network is critical to hope. Did you know that socialization can increase positive feelings and you are 95% more likely to reach a goal if you check in with someone about the goal?

THE HOPE MATRIX™

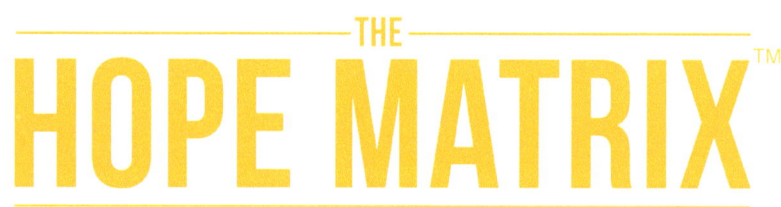

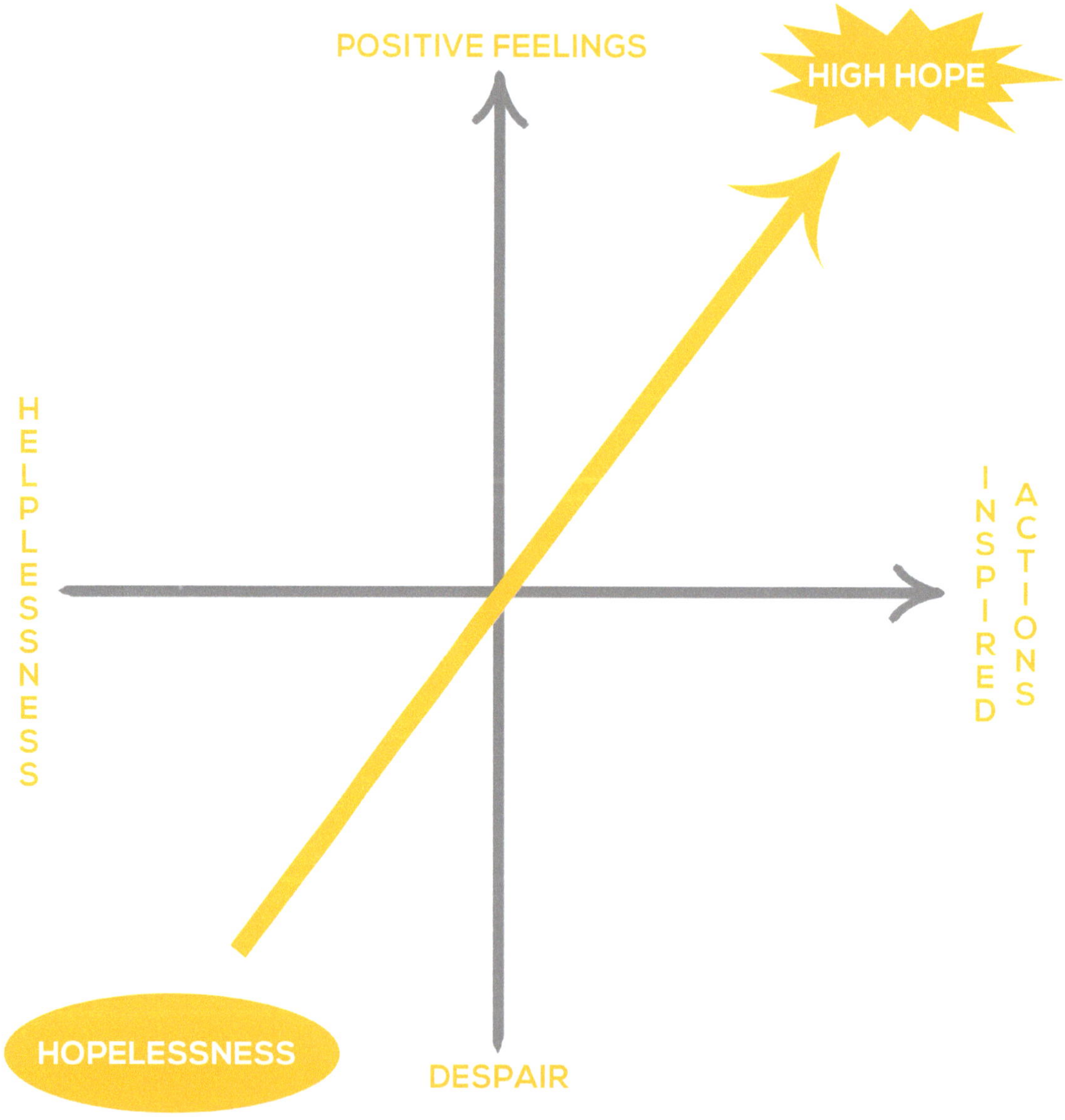
POSITIVE FEELINGS
HIGH HOPE
HELPLESSNESS
INSPIRED ACTIONS
HOPELESSNESS
DESPAIR

WHO ARE YOU HANGING OUT WITH?

Social connection is all about feeling close to other people. It turns out that science says it's super important for us, just like food and water. Our ways of communicating, like facial expressions, tone of voice, and even touch, have evolved to help us build relationships with others.

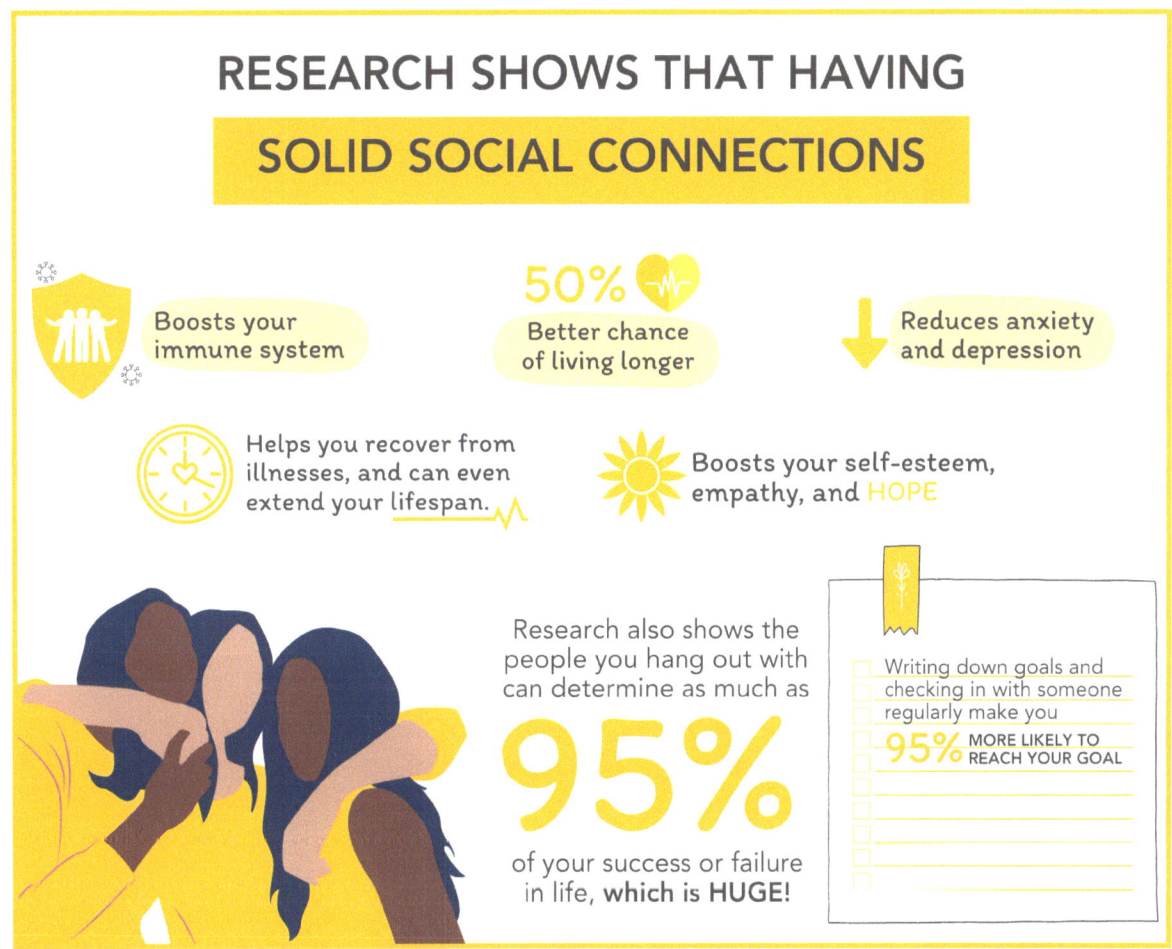

RESEARCH SHOWS THAT HAVING

SOLID SOCIAL CONNECTIONS

Boosts your immune system

50% Better chance of living longer

Reduces anxiety and depression

Helps you recover from illnesses, and can even extend your lifespan.

Boosts your self-esteem, empathy, and HOPE

Research also shows the people you hang out with can determine as much as

95%

of your success or failure in life, **which is HUGE!**

Writing down goals and checking in with someone regularly make you **95%** MORE LIKELY TO REACH YOUR GOAL

SELF-REFLECTION

☀ *What are the goals you want to be successful at?*

☀ *What characteristics are needed to meet those goals (i.e., studying, showing up to class on time, extra curricular activities, etc).*

☀ *Do the people in your social group have these same characteristics?*

Healthy strong relationships can make you healthier both physically and mentally. However, unhealthy relationships can have the opposite effect, so it's important to recognize the signs of unhealthy relationships.

 ## GROUP DISCUSSION

Relationships can be healthy or unhealthy. Check out this article on Psych Central on the signs of toxic relationships. It is true with friends, too. Look at this article in Psychology Today about 8 signs of a toxic friendship.

☀ *Have you ever been in an unhealthy relationship? If so, what were the signs?*

☀ *What about an unhealthy friendship? Have you ever thought about if your friendships were healthy?*

HEALTHY BREAKUPS

Navigating a breakup can be tough, whether it's with a friend or a significant other. Breakups disrupt our routines and challenge our preference for consistency, making it a challenging experience. Breakups can also bring up hopelessness and subsequent anxiety and depression. To help navigate breakups in a healthy way, consider the following:

1. Feel Your Feelings: Breakups bring a wave of emotions that may not feel pleasant, but avoiding them only prolongs the healing process. Allow yourself the time and space to experience and understand the emotions tied to the breakup. Consider expressing your feelings through journaling or deep reflection. You can also turn to your Stress Skills to navigate the emotions that come up.

2. Talk with Friends: Having a strong Nourishing Network is crucial during tough times. Reach out to healthy friends or family members to share your thoughts and feelings about the breakup. Discussing your reactions and processing your emotions with someone you trust can be a cathartic experience, providing a fresh perspective and emotional release.

3. Find Closure: Closure is an essential step in putting the breakup behind you and returning to your normal routine. Closure can take various forms; some people find returning belongings or deleting contact information to be concrete acts of closure. Others may achieve closure by acknowledging the end of the relationship in their minds. Discover what works best for you and helps you acknowledge and accept the conclusion of the relationship.

Remember, healing from a breakup is a unique journey, and it's okay to take the time you need to recover. Following these tips can guide you toward a healthier recovery process and set the foundation for future emotional well-being, while also helping you move back into hope.

GROUP DISCUSSION

☀ *How have you navigated a breakup in the past? What healthy skills did you use?*

☀ *Are there any other healthy breakup tips you can think of as a group?*

IDENTIFYING YOUR HOPE NETWORK

The Fourth Key to Shine Hope is Nourishing Networks, which is your network of individuals you trust and can turn to in times of challenges.

Your hope skills help you overcome challenges to hope, such as worry, rumination, depression, failure, loneliness, and hopelessness. However, even when your hope is strong, there are times when you may still need help.

PEOPLE IN YOUR HOPE NETWORK

Your Nourishing Network can be made up of family members, teachers, friends, neighbors, mentors, siblings, doctors, a divine presence, spiritual leaders, loved ones who have passed, hope heroes, or even pets! Anyone who you can turn to when you are feeling hopeless belongs in your Hope Network. You need to trust them, and they need to be positive influences in your life.

The goal is to surround yourself with people you trust, who will help you through challenging times while supporting you as you work towards your goals.

OTHER ADDITIONS TO YOUR NOURISHING NETWORK

Your Nourishing Network can also include loved ones who have passed or a divine spiritual presence (i.e., God, Buddha, etc.). Drawing strength from the memories of departed loved ones or from spiritual practice can guide us during tough times. Reflecting on their resilience inspires courage in facing our own challenges and can bring comfort, motivation, and renewed purpose to overcome obstacles.

 **GROUP ACTIVITY**

☀ *In this activity, titled "Map of Support," you will create a visual representation of your Nourishing Network. Have everyone grab a piece of paper, markers, and sticky notes. Reflect on your own Nourishing Network and write down the names of three people, pets, or spiritual presences on separate sticky notes. Then, write down a sentence or two on how they fit into your Nourishing Network. Share your choices with the group, explaining why you chose them. Place the sticky notes on the board, arranging them creatively. Discuss commonalities, surprises, and ways to strengthen your support network. Display the completed map as a reminder of the importance of support.*

☀ *Who can you draw strength from during times of loneliness?*

☀ *Before we continue, if you feel comfortable doing so, indicate whether you are willing to be part of someone's Nourishing Network. This means being there to offer support and encouragement when they need it. It's like being a friend they can rely on during tough times. Don't worry; it's okay if you don't want to commit to this right now.*

☀ *Who is one person who you may be able to go to for support?*

DEVELOPING YOUR NOURISHING NETWORK

Unfortunately, as our society has changed and grown, we've started to lose some of social connections. It's tough because we naturally yearn for social interaction. That's why it's no surprise that we all experience feelings of loneliness at times. In fact, in 2021, a staggering **61%** of teenagers reported feeling lonely often.

When you're lonely, it messes with your thoughts and changes the chemicals in your brain. It can make your brain produce more cortisol, which is the stress hormone. And too much cortisol can have negative effects on your physical health, downstairs brain, and increase moments of hopelessness.

But here's the thing: Hope is a powerful tool in combating loneliness and creating a sense of belonging because it puts you in control of your situation. Hope gives you a fresh perspective on the future by helping you set specific goals that you truly want to achieve. It's about looking forward and envisioning a better tomorrow. And along the way, hope also prepares you for any obstacles or challenges you might face.

 **GROUP DISCUSSION**

☀ *How can you create relationships with people? Where can you meet people who have the characteristics you identified earlier?*

☀ *How can you find someone that you can count on in times of challenges?*

☀ *What are strategies you can use to create friendships?*

You may find that you struggle to identify someone who is in your Hope Network. It is important to remember that Hope Networks are not fixed; they will continue to grow and change each and every day. As you make your way through the exercise, and even throughout the school year, remember to keep reaching out to keep building a strong Hope Network.

It is also important to identify faculty/staff within your school, such as the school nurse, social worker, or counselor, that you can reach out to in times of need.

 # GROUP DISCUSSION

Discuss hopelessness and how it gets in the way of making connections with others. Problem-solve as a group on how to overcome hopelessness as a barrier for connection.

Begin to brainstorm the people who belong in your Nourishing Network and were they fit:

Friends and family I count on:

People I turn to for Stress Skills:

People I practice Happiness Habits with:

Things I can connect to (e.g. Spiritual advisor, peer support, pets, nature, etc.):

Medical experts I can turn to when I need help:

Community resources I can utilize:

Places I can go in times of crisis:

STRENGTHENING YOUR HOPE NETWORK

It is critical to not just have a Hope Network but to strengthen your network. Relationships take work, time, and energy. When you feel lonely, your first inclination may be to withdraw. However, that can create more loneliness. When you feel alone, it's important to reach out and continue to foster your relationships. Strengthen your Hope Network by actively working on your relationship with the people within your Hope Network.

You can enhance your Hope Network with:

5:1 Rule: In healthy relationships, like the ones you should have with the people in your Hope Network, you should exchange **five positive comments** for every constructive criticism or negative comments. You may find that using this ratio is harder than it seems. Like everything else you do in this course, the 5:1 rule may take practice to achieve.

Think of someone in your Hope Network. In the space below, write down five things you appreciate about them:

As your inspired action for this lesson, consider reaching out to the person above and telling them the five things you wrote down.

GROUP DISCUSSION

☀ *Do you feel like you follow the 5:1 rule with the people in your Hope Network? When is it most challenging to follow? Why?*

☀ *How can you improve your ratio?*

What is vulnerability? How do we express vulnerability? What are examples of vulnerability in your life?

Have you opened up and been vulnerable with someone in the past? How did it make you feel? How did it impact your relationship with that person?

Praise and Recognition: Acknowledging another person's strengths or accomplishments shows them you care. When you raise up the people in your Hope Networks, they in turn raise you up.

Brainstorm people in your Hope Network who deserve your praise or recognition

How do praise and recognition help to strengthen your relationship with others?

Kindness: When you perform an act of kindness, it not only bolsters your hope; it also positively affects the hope of the person on the receiving end, and the hope of anyone who witnesses it. These acts of kindness also enhance your relationships with people within your Hope Network.

GROUP DISCUSSION

Have you seen any acts of kindness recently? What were they? How did they make you feel? How did the people who received them react?

Gratitude: The people in your Hope Network are people who support you and help you succeed. It is important to not only acknowledge their support but also show them how much you appreciate it.

Write down three people in your Hope Network and why you are grateful for them:

1. _____
   _____

2. _____
   _____

3. _____
   _____

As your inspired action for this lesson, consider reaching out to the people above and telling them why you're grateful for them.

Empathy: The empathy you give and receive from the relationships with the people around you provides an emotional connection and support system while reducing your feelings of worry, stress, loneliness, and hopelessness.

 ## GROUP DISCUSSION

☀ *How can you make it easier to give or receive empathy?*

☀ *Why is empathy sometimes difficult to give or receive?*

☀ *How can you show empathy to people in your Hope Network? What does empathy look like?*

PUTTING MYSELF IN THEIR SHOES

Directions: Fill in each blank below with 1-5 words or emotions.

THE LAST TIME SOMEONE WAS UNKIND TO ME:

_____

_____

HOW I FELT:

_____

_____

HOW THEY MIGHT HAVE FELT:

_____

_____

HOW THEY COULD HAVE SHOWN EMPATHY:

_____

_____

HOW I COULD HAVE SHOWN EMPATHY:

_____

_____

THE LAST TIME I WAS UNKIND TO SOMEONE ELSE:

_____

_____

HOW I FELT:

_____

_____

HOW THEY MIGHT HAVE FELT:

_____

_____

HOW THEY COULD HAVE SHOWN EMPATHY:

_____

_____

HOW I COULD HAVE SHOWN EMPATHY:

_____

_____

Compassion, Forgiveness, and Self-Forgiveness: Forgiveness is one of the key ways that you show empathy to the people around you. Forgiveness is when you release the negative emotions, such as anger, sadness, or frustration, that are associated with an action that another person (or your former self) has made. Forgiveness is larger than simply saying, "it's okay" when someone apologizes; it is a conscious decision to release your negative emotions and return to a hopeful mindset.

Are you holding on to negative emotions about yourself or someone else? Why? What is the first step you can take to begin releasing those negative emotions and practicing forgiveness?

NURTURING NETWORKS AND HOPE:
TYING IT ALL TOGETHER

Nurturing Networks create a sense of belongingness, which is deeply interconnected with hope, especially for teenagers. When individuals feel a strong sense of belonging, it fosters a positive environment that nurtures hope. Belongingness provides a support system where individuals feel understood, valued, and supported by others.

This sense of connection and support is crucial in maintaining hope during difficult times. When faced with challenges or setbacks, knowing that you belong to a community or have a network of supportive relationships gives you the confidence and reassurance that you are not alone.

HOPE HERO SPOTLIGHT

BTS

Korean pop (K-pop) band BTS has distinguished themselves as one of the most internationally-acclaimed Korean bands of all time. Despite the majority of their songs being sung in Korean, people around the world have joined the BTS "ARMY" of fans.

While BTS is known for their strong social media presence and iconic dance moves and music videos, it is their focus on friendship and social connection that sets them apart. Throughout their rise to fame, BTS has continually spoken about the importance of their connection to each other, their families, and their friends. BTS understands that their strong Hope Network keeps them focused, hopeful, and in their creative upstairs brains.

BTS extends this Hope Network to their fans as well. They've used their influence to help those who may not have a strong Hope Network of their own. Through their speeches about hope and connection in the United States General Assembly, their Love Myself campaign, and their continual support of marginalized communities, BTS aims to remind every single person that they are never alone.

In the wake of the COVID-19 pandemic, BTS has worked hard to connect with young people around the world and inspire hope. In fact, their most recent appearance at the United States General Assembly was focused on that:

https://www.unicef.org/lac/en/BTS-LoveMyself

Unlike BTS, most of us cannot create Hope Networks on a global scale. However, we can use their example to foster our own Hope Networks and remember that, no matter how lonely we feel, we are never truly alone.*

*This story was created from publicly available information. It does not suggest endorsement of Hopeful Minds, or any affiliation by known celebrity to our program. All information is for illustrative purposes for youth, to demonstrate skills used to create, maintain, and grow hope.

LESSON TAKEAWAY (GROUP DISCUSSION):

☀ *What is one piece of information you found most helpful in this lesson?*

☀ *How will you incorporate the information you learned in this lesson to your life this week?*

☀ *BTS used their influence to create a global Hope Network. What is one specific method they used to enhance their relationships with others?*

Go back to the very first worksheet on page 11, where you identified your hope hero. Fill in the individuals that are in your hope hero's Nourishing Network.

WEEKLY HOPE ACTIVATION

Inspired Actions for Hope are the things you can do to reinforce these lessons and begin to bring hope skills into your daily life. Choose at least one of the actions below to complete before moving to the next lesson.

☀ 5:1 Rule- challenge yourself to use the 5:1 rule all week. Keep track of your progress and identify people in your life with whom you don't keep the ratio.

☀ Complete random acts of kindness to three people.

☀ Reach out to someone in your Hope Network and set up a time to do something fun with them.

NOTES

Post your completed activities on social media using the following hashtags to help us teach the lessons. Make sure to tag us **@ifredorg** and **@theshinehopecompany.**

#HopefulMindsTeens #Hope #ShineHope #ScienceofHope #NourishingNetworks #HopeNetwork #MyOnePerson (and have them tag there one person) #Gratitude #Kindness

NOURISHING NETWORKS

Your Nourishing Networks, also known as your Hope Networks, are the people in your life that provide you with support, help you stay on track, encourage you to succeed, and who you do the same for in return. You are up to 95% more likely to achieve a goal if you write it down, and check in with someone regularly. So Nourishing Networks are critical support systems for moving you towards what you hope for in life.

Your Hope Networks should include:

People who know and understand you.

People who value your strengths.

People who activate the SHINE framework.

People whom you trust and can confide in.

People who are available to support you.

People you are willing to do the above for as well.

Enhancing Your Hope Networks

Enhance your Hope Networks using the 5:1 rule, vulnerability, praise, recognition, kindness, gratitude, empathy, compassion, collaboration, and strong communication, and be sure to have different networks for different areas of life.

Don't forget to include doctors, therapists, and/or other medical professionals in your Hope Networks.

Module 10:
The Fifth Key to Shine Hope: Eliminating Challenges

Module 10:
The Fifth Key to Shine Hope: Eliminating Challenges

The fifth and final key to Shine Hope is Eliminating Challenges, which are the obstacles that can cause despair and motivational helplessness. It's important to identify ways to manage challenges before they arise so you can quickly and easily move from moments of hopelessness back to hope.

CHALLENGES TO HOPE

Obstacles are an inevitable part of life, and they can bring up down and prevent up from feeling hopeful. These obstacles are called "Challenges to Hope," and they're like negative thinking habits that lead us to feel hopeless and helpless. The tricky thing is that these thought patterns are often unconscious, so we don't even realize we're doing them. That's why it's crucial to become aware of these patterns. Once we know what they are and recognize them, we can take action to counteract them.
By doing this, we can make sure these challenges don't hold us back from all the amazing things we hope for in life.

Challenge #1: Limiting Beliefs

Limiting beliefs are negative thoughts or opinions that you tell yourself are true that keep you in a negative mindset. Examples: **"I'm not smart enough to succeed in that field." "I'm not attractive enough to find love."**

Challenge #2: Automatic Negative Thoughts

Automatic negative thoughts, or ANTs, are unpleasant thoughts that pop up in our minds automatically when something happens around us. Examples: **"Nobody likes me," "I'm so stupid." "I'm a failure."**

Challenge #3: All-or-Nothing Thinking

All-or-nothing thinking is when we see things in extreme ways, without considering any middle ground. It's like thinking in black and white, with no shades of gray in between. Example: **"If I don't get. perfect score on the test, I'm a failure."**

Challenge #4: Negative Bias

Negative bias occurs when we fixate on negative events more than positive events. Examples: **Focusing on one critical comment rather than the positive feedback, or discounting positive experiences.**

Challenge #5: Rumination

Rumination refers to when you repeatedly go over a thought or a problem from the past in your head, without end. Example: **Constantly replaying and analyzing past mistakes**

Challenge #6: Uncontrollables

Focusing on Uncontrollables is when you focus on things that are outside of your influence of power. Examples: **How others react to a situation or past events you have experienced.**

Challenge #7: Attaching to Outcomes

Attaching to outcomes is when you set goals, and are then unable or willing to be satisfied unless you reach that specific goal. Example: **Becoming attached to acceptance at a particular college**

Challenge #8: Internalizing Failure

Taking personal responsibility for failure or setback. If failure affects your emotions and confidence you are more likely to make future mistakes. Example: **Blaming yourself for a poor grade on a test you studied hard for.**

There are many threats to hope that we face in our day-to-day lives, such as the news. The news chooses negative headlines as this was the norm in the past, to search for threats. The news has capitalized on this, yet seeing negative things over and over can increase worry and rumination.

 ## GROUP DISCUSSION

☀ *Why does the news cover negative stories?*

☀ *Discuss how the news makes you feel?*
Brainstorm as a group how you can take your power back as it relates to the news.

GROUP ACTIVITY

Read the vignettes below and discuss which challenges these teens are facing. (Hint: each vignette includes three separate challenges).

Vignette # 1: Emily

As the final bell rang, signaling the end of the school day, Emily packed her backpack and headed home. She couldn't shake off the unease that had settled in her mind since receiving her English test results that morning. Sitting on the bus, her thoughts started to spiral.

"I can't believe I got a C- on that test," Emily thought to herself. "I'm such a failure. I always mess up when it comes to English. I'll never be good enough."

The bus ride felt longer than usual as Emily fell deeper into her thoughts surrounding the test. She replayed every question she got wrong, obsessing over each mistake, and imagining her teacher's disappointment. "I'm never going to improve. I'm just not smart enough," she whispered to herself.

As she entered her house, Emily's mood continued. Looking at the neatly decorated hallway, she only saw the one picture frame that had slipped slightly to the side. "Nothing ever goes right. Everything is always a mess," she muttered, completely disregarding the beauty of the rest of the hallway.

With a heavy heart, Emily retreated to her room. She collapsed into her bed and said to herself, "If I'm not perfect, then I'm a failure. It's either success or complete disaster. There's no in-between," she thought, unable to see any possibility for improvement or growth.

The evening passed, and Emily's mind continued to spiral about the English test. She became convinced that her score defined her abilities as a student and that she was personally responsible for the grade. She started doubting herself in other areas as well, feeling like she was destined to fail at everything.

Vignette 2: Lily

As the sun dipped below the horizon, casting a warm glow over the park, Lily stood at the edge of the basketball court, nervously bouncing the ball in her hands. The upcoming tryouts for the school basketball team had been consuming her thoughts for weeks, fueling a mix of excitement and anxiety within her.

As she stepped onto the court, her mind became a whirlwind of thoughts about herself. "I'm not tall enough," she thought, glancing at the other players who seemed taller and more confident. "I'm not skilled enough. There's no way I'll make the team."

With every dribble, more and more thoughts automatically came into her mind. "I always mess up under pressure," Lily whispered to herself, feeling the weight of self-doubt. "I'm going to embarrass myself out there. I'm not cut out for this."

As the tryouts commenced, Lily couldn't help but attach her self-worth to the outcome. Every shot she missed, every pass that went awry, fueled her growing belief that she wasn't good enough. Her anxiety heightened, and she desperately tried to control the opinions of the coaches and the outcome of the tryouts.

With each missed shot, Lily's frustration grew. "If I don't make the team, my friends will think I'm a failure," she thought, feeling the weight of others' expectations bearing down on her. "I have to make the team to prove myself."

As the final whistle blew, signaling the end of the tryouts, Lily's heart sank.

GROUP ACTIVITY

Have everyone in the group write down examples of 1-2 challenges they've faced on pieces of paper. Put all the pieces of paper into a pile and have one group member randomly draw from the pile. As a group, label what type of challenge the person was facing.

GROUP DISCUSSION

☀ *Take turns talking about past challenges you've had. How did the challenge impact your ability to meet goals and feel positively charged emotions? How did you work through the challenge?*

ELIMINATING CHALLENGES

THINK THROUGH THE EVIDENCE

A great way to work through challenged thinking is to think about the evidence that goes against the thought. For example, Emily believed she was a failure for earning a B on her English test. There is a lot of evidence that goes against the thought that she's a failure including, (1) she earned a B, which is not classified as a failing grade, (2) she has made her way through school up until this point without any grade retention. And there are likely many more pieces of evidence we could draw out if we had the chance to talk to Emily.

USE YOUR STRESS SKILLS

Challenging thoughts are not fun and can lead to stress, which gives us a perfect opportunity to practice those stress skills. At this point in the Hopeguide, we hope that you've started to identify what stress skills work best for you!

DIALECTICAL THINKING

Dialectical thinking is when two conflicting things are true at the same time, so you take the middle path and accept both. There is always more than one true way to see a situation and two things that are opposite can both be true. For example, I am capable of learning a new topic in school by myself, but I also need support to encourage and motivate me through the process.

This can also come in handy with social relationships. Sometimes both people are right about something, even if it seems that their opinions are completely opposite. For example, in a movie one friend may view the main character as a hero and the other friend may view the main character as the villain. Both those viewpoints can be accurate.

REMEMBER YOUR PURPOSE

Purpose instills a sense of hope, as it represents a vision of a better future. It reminds individuals that their efforts are not in vain and that they have the potential to make a positive impact. Remembering their purpose in challenging moments can help people maintain a hopeful outlook, believing that they can overcome obstacles and create meaningful change.

PRACTICE YOUR HAPPINESS HABITS

Remember that Happiness Habits help keep us in the upstairs brain, so continue to practice those every day!

WORKSHEET

Complete the statements below with your personal strategies for overcoming the challenges discussed in this lesson. For more ideas on how to overcome challenges, see an example of the completed worksheet below.

When I'm experiencing Limiting Beliefs, my strategy to overcome this challenge is to

When I'm experiencing Automatic Negative Thoughts, my strategy to overcome this challenge is to

When I'm experiencing All-or-Nothing thinking, my strategy to overcome this challenge is to

When I experience Negative Bias, my strategy to overcome this challenge is to

When I experience Rumination, my strategy to overcome this challenge is to

When I experience Attachment to Outcomes, my strategy to overcome this challenge is to

When I experience Internalizing Failure, my strategy to overcome this challenge is to

Examples:

When I'm experiencing Limiting Beliefs, my strategy to overcome this challenge is to

> **remember my purpose and think through the evidence.**

When I'm experiencing Automatic Negative Thoughts, my strategy to overcome this challenge is to

> **practice stress skills and think through the evidence.**

When I'm experiencing All-or-Nothing thinking, my strategy to overcome this challenge is to

> **practice dialectical thinking.**

When I experience Negative Bias, my strategy to overcome this challenge is to

> **practice my happiness habits.**

When I experience Rumination, my strategy to overcome this challenge is to

> **practice my stress skills.**

When I experience Attachment to Outcomes, my strategy to overcome this challenge is to

> **practice dialectical thinking.**

When I experience Internalizing Failure, my strategy to overcome this challenge is to

> **think through the evidence and remember my purpose.**

 Discuss the worksheet and each member's plans for overcoming the challenges.

ELIMINATING CHALLENGES AND HOPE:
TYING EVERYTHING TOGETHER

Challenges are a natural part of life, and we can't expect them to disappear completely. But here's the thing: Hope is what keeps us going even when things get tough. It's about believing that positive outcomes are possible, even in the face of difficulties.

Hope gives us the optimism and belief that we can find solutions, make progress, and achieve our goals. It helps us see challenges as temporary hurdles rather than impossible roadblocks. So, let's embrace challenges as opportunities for growth, and remember that hope is our secret weapon to keep pushing forward, no matter what comes our way.

HOPE HERO SPOTLIGHT

SELENA GOMEZ

In 2014, singer and actress Selena Gomez was diagnosed with lupus. Lupus is a disease that causes someone's immune system to attack their own body. Selena's lupus caused her physical pain; it hurt her stomach, made her skin break out in rashes, and made her hands and feet swell and throb. It also gave her anxiety, panic attacks, and depression.

Selena's diagnosis was a challenge she had to face and it would have been easy for her to fall into a hopelessness cycle. Instead, Selena focused on the things she could control. She couldn't control her diagnosis, but she could focus on the things she could do to minimize her symptoms. Selena established a routine, improved her diet, and worked with her doctors to find the correct medications for her symptoms.

 When the lupus got worse, Selena's kidneys began to shut down. Her doctors told her that if she couldn't find someone to give her a kidney, she would die. It would have once again been easy for Selena to give up. Thankfully, when she felt overwhelmed with hopelessness, Selena knew what she needed to do; he asked for help. Instead of falling into a worry spiral, she relied on her Hope Network to help her stay hopeful.

Her Nourishing Network supported her, helped bolster her spirits, and her friend, Francia Raisa, even gave Selena one of her kidneys. Like Selena, we will all face obstacles in our lives that we cannot control. However, by focusing on the things we can control, using our hope skills, and relying on our Nourishing Networks, there is no obstacle we cannot handle.*

This story was created from publicly available information. It does not suggest endorsement of Hopeful Minds, or any affiliation by known celebrity to our program. All information is for illustrative purposes for youth, to demonstrate skills used to create, maintain, and grow hope.

☀ *What is one piece of information you found most helpful in this lesson?*

☀ *How will you incorporate the information you learned in this lesson to your life this week?*

☀ *What are other ways Selena used the Shine Hope framework to combat her experience of hopelessness? (With permission, you can search online if needed).*

Go back to the very first worksheet on page 11, where you identified your hope hero. Fill in how your hope hero has Eliminated Challenges.

WEEKLY HOPE ACTIVATION

Inspired Actions for Hope are the things you can do to reinforce these lessons and begin to bring hope skills into your daily life. Choose at least one of the actions below to complete before moving to the next lesson.

☀ When you feel yourself entering a rumination or worry cycle, attach to outcomes, internalize failure, or focus on the uncontrollables, take a 90-second pause and use your favorite Stress Skill to return to the present moment and your upstairs brain.

☀ Continue to practice replacing limiting beliefs, ANTs, and negative biases with reaffirming beliefs and a cultivated hope.

☀ Control the controllables Worksheet (Next page)

Answer Key:
Vignette 1 includes rumination (paragraph 3), all-or-nothing thinking (paragraph 5), negative bias (paragraph 4), and internalizing failure (paragraph 5).

Vignette 2 including automatic negative thoughts (paragraph 3), attaching to outcomes (paragraph 5), trying to control the uncontrollables (paragraph 4), and limiting beliefs (paragraph 2).

CONTROL THE CONTROLLABLES

Directions: List or draw the things you CAN control in the space inside the sunflower. List or draw the things you CAN'T control in the space around the sunflower.

THINGS THAT I CAN'T CONTROL

THINGS THAT I CAN CONTROL

NOTES

Post your completed activities on social media using the following hashtags to help us teach the lessons. Make sure to tag us **@ifredorg** and **@theshinehopecompany.**

#HopefulMindsTeens #Hope #ShineHope #ScienceofHope
#EliminatingChallenges #ControlTheUncontrollables

ELIMINATING CHALLENGES

Challenges to Hope are negative habits of thought that quickly take you to hopelessness, that emotional despair and sense of helplessness. The thought patterns are often unconscious habits, so becoming aware of these patterns is critical. Once we know what they are and recognize them, it is important to counteract them so that we don't let them keep us from all we hope for in life.

Eliminating Challenges

Most of the Challenges to Hope take constant, repetitive actions to change and overcome. Thanks to the science of neuroplasticity, we know it is possible with practice and dedication. The key is to learn to identify what specific challenges happen most frequently and then proactively find ways to manage those challenges.

Limiting beliefs	Focusing on Uncontrollables	Mind Wandering
Automatic Negative Thoughts (ANTs)	Attaching to outcomes	Implicit Bias
All-or-nothing thinking	Internalizing failure	Negative Framing
Negative bias	Toxic Consumption	Perfectionism
Rumination & Worry	Nocebo Effect	Taking things personally

Module 11:
Using Resources to Shine

Module 11: Using Resources to Shine

The Five Keys to Shine Hope are a set of skills that can be reinforced by the resources in your environment. We want to ensure that the resources we access are supplementing our positive feelings and inspired actions rather than leading us closer to despair and motivational helplessness.

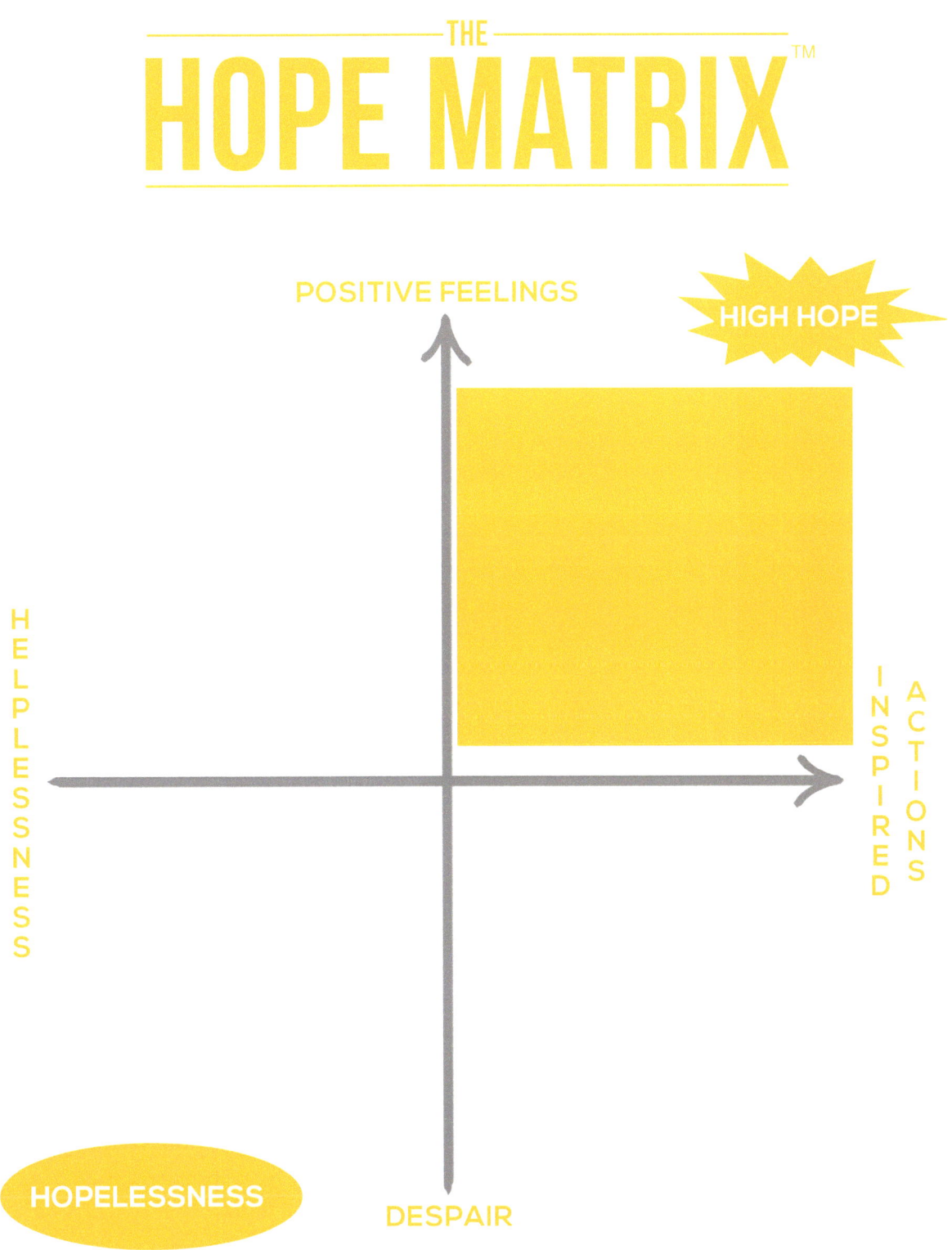

It's no secret that our society is ruled by technology. Everything involves a screen now. Need to write a school paper? You'll pull out your laptop and start typing. Going out with friends? You'll use your phone to coordinate with your friends and possibly rely on it for directions to get to the event. You are probably using technology for this program.

Technology brings a multitude of benefits to teenagers. Firstly, it provides easy access to information, allowing us to expand our knowledge and learn about diverse topics. It enables us to connect with friends, family, and like-minded individuals through social media and messaging apps, fostering relationships and a sense of belonging.

Technology offers a platform for self-expression, creativity, and showcasing talents through various digital mediums. It simplifies and enhances our learning experiences through educational apps, online courses, and interactive tools. Additionally, technology opens doors to new opportunities, whether it's exploring career paths, starting online businesses, or advocating for causes we believe in.

Even if you have forgotten your phone at home, the world is still filled with screens. Technology is beautiful, and it has certainly contributed to many conveniences and connections we can all appreciate (I'm using multiple forms of technology as I type up this lesson!)

 **GROUP DISCUSSION**

☀ *Discuss your experiences with technology, including how technology has helped you and what you like about technology.*

GROUP ACTIVITY

With parent permission, search the internet for articles that discuss the benefits of technology and use the space below to list a few of the benefits you find in your search. Look for articles that come from reputable sources, such as academic institutions (i.e., universities or colleges), government organizations (i.e., CDC), medical institutions (i.e., Mayo Clinic, WebMD), nonprofit organizations (i.e., WHO, Redcross), professional organizations (i.e., APA, AMA), or research journals (i.e., ncbi.nlm.nih.gov).

It's unrealistic to think that technology is going away or becoming stagnant. Each and every day, greater technological advances are popping up. As great as technology is, we can also note that there are times when technology isn't so helpful. Remember dialectical thinking from the last lesson? We are allowed to both appreciate technology and notice how it can impact our lives.

GROUP DISCUSSION

☀ *Discuss times in your life when you've found technology distracting or unhelpful.*

☀ *Read through the following two articles and then answer the following prompts:*
What are your thoughts on these articles? How do they relate to the information you've already learned in this lesson about screen time?
    1. *https://gabb.com/blog/how-smart-phones-affect-brain-development/*
    2. *https://gabb.com/blog/austin-weirichs-story/*

With parent permission, search the internet for articles that discuss the screen time and the brain. Then, reflect on the following questions:

What did you find out about screen time?

What do researchers say about a lot of screen time?

Were you surprised by your findings?

What did you learn about the positive or negative effects of screen time?

WORKSHEET

Understanding Technology Worksheet.

What pieces of technology with screens do you use every day?

Which pieces of technology are required for school or work? Which are recreational? Which are both?

How much time, on average, do you spend on each piece of technology?

Are you satisfied with this number?　◯ YES　◯ NO

Why or why not?

LET'S GET SOCIAL

Navigating screen time can be challenging, especially when it comes to social media and texting. You know that feeling when you get a notification on your phone? It's like a little reward for your brain, releasing dopamine, which makes you feel good. And that's why we keep coming back for more. But here's the thing, even when we don't have any notifications, we still find ourselves checking our phones and scrolling through social media.

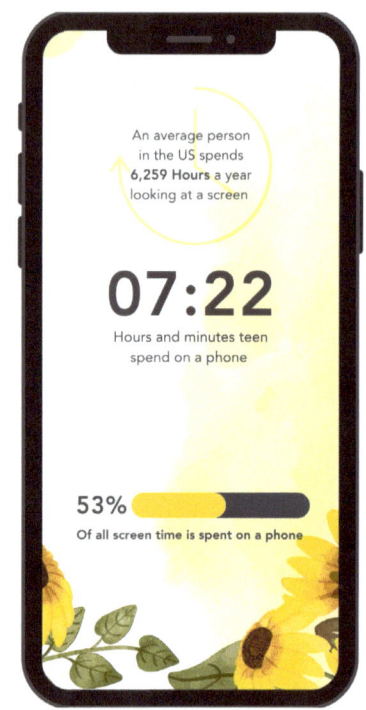

An average person in the US spends **6,259 Hours** a year looking at a screen

07:22
Hours and minutes teen spend on a phone

53%
Of all screen time is spent on a phone

Social media is designed to keep us hooked and can even cause us to become addicted through something called intermittent reinforcement. The notifications we get are random, and that's what makes it even more addictive. We hope that each time we check our phones, we'll get that dopamine rush. It's like a gamble, and we keep playing the game. But here's the catch: this constant need for validation and the fear of missing out (FOMO) can lead to comparing ourselves to others and feeling down about our own lives.

 ## GROUP ACTIVITY

☀ *There is a famous set of studies in the 1970s led by Bruce Alexander called "rat park," that highlight the link between social connection and the likelihood of addiction. With your parents permission, look for YouTube videos and articles about rat park to learn more about the studies. Then, as a group, talk about how these studies may or may not relate to social media use.*

☀ *One important finding from addiction-related studies is that once we are addicted to something (i.e., food, screens, substances, etc.), it's much harder to break that addiction, and once the brain has become addicted to one thing, it's easier for addiction to transfer to another addiction. Therefore, it's important to recognize signs of emerging addictions to break the cycle before it leads to negative consequences.*

Another thing to consider is that social media can be a tricky place. It's filled with carefully curated images and content that is meant to get as many likes as possible. We see these perfect versions of people's lives, and it's easy to feel left out or inadequate if we're going through our own challenges. It can make us feel lonely and hopeless, and that's when things like depression, anxiety, and even thoughts of suicide can creep in.

So, it's important to be mindful of how much time we spend on our phones and social media. It's okay to take breaks and disconnect from the online world. Remember that what you see on social media is just a highlight reel, not the full story. Focus on your own journey, and don't let social media dictate your happiness. If you ever find yourself feeling overwhelmed or struggling with your mental health, reach out to someone you trust, whether it's a friend, family member, or professional. You're not alone, and there is support available to help you through tough times.

 **GROUP DISCUSSION**

☀ *What has been your experience with social media? What do you like and dislike about it?*

☀ *What are the main reasons you like to use social media?*

☀ *What type of content do you engage with on social media and what does it do to your hope level?*

☀ *Do you feel the need to present yourself a certain way online?*

☀ *How do you feel when you come across someone on social media whom you admire and would like to be more like?*

☀ *When witnessing bullying on social media what can you do to help the other person? If you are being bullied on social media, what steps can you take to protect your mental health?*

MAKING A PLAN FOR TECHNOLOGY

It's important to recognize that completely cutting off social media and phone usage may not be realistic or necessary. They have become a big part of our lives. However, if you feel down or overwhelmed when using your phone or social media, you have control to take steps toward how you use technology.

 **GROUP ACTIVITY**

Step 1: *Using the chart below, write out healthy ways to use technology and unhealthy ways to use technology.*

Step 2: *Once you've completed the list, discuss some strategies to protect yourself from these unhealthy ways of using technology.*

Healthy	Unhealthy

Check the signs that you notice in yourself when technology causes you to feel overwhelmed.

○ Sadness   ○ Losing sleep

○ Anxiety   ○ Excessively checking technology

○ Isolating from friends/family   ○ Poor self-esteem

○ Other: _____

GROUP DISCUSSION

 *Discuss ways someone can implement healthy strategies for their technology use if they notice themselves feeling down or overwhelmed by their use.*

HOPE AND TECHNOLOGY

Technology plays a crucial role in inspiring hope in many ways. First, it gives us access to endless information, helping us learn and discover new possibilities. It connects us with people from all over the world, creating communities where we can find support and encouragement.

Technology also fuels innovation, solving big problems and showing us that challenges can be overcome. It empowers us to pursue our passions, express ourselves, and make a positive impact. How technology is used can be customized to meet the needs of its user, so figure out what works best for your life.

ED SHEERAN

The musician Ed Sheeran is very familiar with using his hope skills and taking social media breaks. Most celebrities are bombarded by messages across social media platforms, which gives open opportunities for criticism. Ed realized quickly into his career that constantly checking social media and reading the messages didn't maintain positive feelings, and there were many times when he felt more sad than happy while scrolling through social media.

Instead of continuing to check social media to get more of those intermittent dopamine spikes, Ed decided to use his Stress Skills of building with legos and Happiness Habits of traveling to new places, which allowed him to reach his music production goals.

Ed first took a break from social media in 2016 after winning a Grammy. He told magazines he went to Japan to "eat weird food, soak in the hot springs and ski," which are Ed's happiness habits. Since then, Ed continues to use his stress skills by stepping away from social media when he needs a break.

Ed didn't just wish social media would stop making him feel sad; he hoped to feel more connected to his nourishing network, so he used his stress skills and happiness habits to help take a break from social media and build hope.*

This story was created from publicly available information. It does not suggest endorsement of Hopeful Minds, or any affiliation by known celebrity to our program. All information is for illustrative purposes for youth, to demonstrate skills used to create, maintain, and grow hope.

☀ *What is one piece of information you found most helpful in this lesson?*

☀ *How will you incorporate the information you learned in this lesson to your life this week?*

☀ *Ed Sheeran gives us an example of what a social media break can look like. What do you think would happen if Ed didn't take social media breaks?*

☀ *Think about your Hope Hero from the start of the Hopeguide; what do you think of their technology habits? How does your Hope Hero's technology habits influence you?*

WEEKLY HOPE ACTIVATION

Inspired Actions for Hope are the things you can do to reinforce these lessons and begin to bring hope skills into your daily life. Choose at least one of the actions below to complete before moving to the next lesson.

☀ Develop a plan on what you'll do if technology begins to make you experience hopelessness.

☀ Set SMART goals around your technology usage.

☀ Track how much time you spend on your phone for one day. Consider if the usage is improving your hope. If not, challenge yourself to make a change in your phone use the next day.

☀ Use technology to help you learn how to overcome an obstacle (*i.e. college admission; improving at sports, etc.*).

☀ *Check out resources to see different perspectives of technology use.*

Post your completed activities on social media using the following hashtags to help us teach the lessons. Make sure to tag us **@ifredorg** and **@theshinehopecompany.**

#HopefulMinds #Teens #Hope #ShineHope #HopeScience #HopeSkills

Module 12:
Creating a Vision for your Future to Shine Hope

Module 12: Creating a Vision for your Future to Shine Hope

CONTINUING YOUR HOPE JOURNEY

As you reach the final lesson of this course, it's important to understand that hope is way more than just a simple "wish." Hope is both a thought and an action that requires practice.

The journey doesn't end here. You've begun to cultivate hope, but just like any other skill, you need to practice your Five Keys to Shine Hope every day through practice and activation based on the strategies provided in this Hopeguide. The more you do it, the easier it becomes, and the more natural the hopeful mindset becomes in your everyday life.

Today, we're going to discuss the tools you can use to keep growing in your own hope journey, as well as ways to inspire hope in your community. Even after completing this course, you can always come back to this list to keep enhancing your hope skills and spreading the message of hope worldwide.

RETAKE THE HOPE SCALE

During the first lesson of this course, you took the Snyder Hope Assessment to measure your level of hope. Use the link provided or scan the QR code (Page 196) and retake the assessment now that you are at the end of the course.

www.hopefulminds.org/hope-scales
www.theshinehopecompany.com/measure-your-hope

Now, using the blank graph below, plot your hope score from lesson one and your hope score from today.

My Hope Score Change

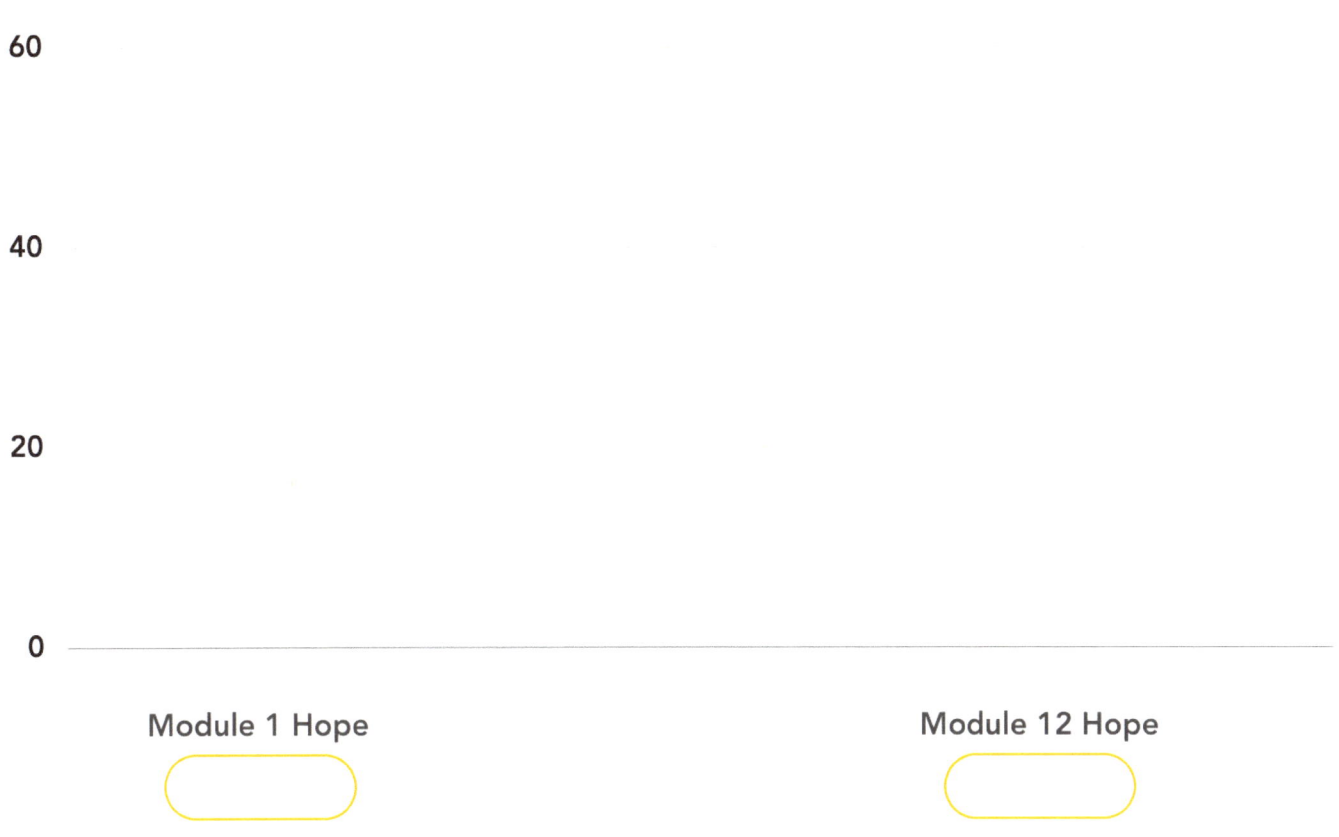

60	
40	
20	
0	

Module 1 Hope   Module 12 Hope

If your hope score went up
Great! You're well on your way to cultivate hope and can gain a lot of positive health and academic outcomes with higher hope.

If your hope score went down
Don't give up! We all face rough patches in life and sometimes those rough patches can be tough to get through. This Hopeguide is just the beginning of your journey. Keep practicing those hope skills we went over in this Hopeguide and before you know it, your hope score can rise!

☀ *Discuss the change in your Hope score. What do you think caused your Hope score to change?*

☀ *Do you feel you have the tools necessary to raise your hope even more? How can the group support each other in continuing to raise each other's hope?*

These days, there's a ton of stress going on in the world, and a lot of it is completely out of our hands. No wonder feelings of hopelessness are on the rise. But here's the thing: because there are so many things we can't control, it's crucial for us to be super focused on practicing and honing our hope skills. We need to break free from our stress mode and reconnect with positive emotions. Instead of feeling helpless, we should channel our energy into taking inspired actions.

ACTIVATING HOPE

The best way to improve and inspire your own hope is to activate it in your life and your community. When you engage in volunteering activities, it not only benefits others but also has a positive impact on yourself. People who have volunteered often share that it boosts their self-confidence, self-esteem, and even brings them good luck.

According to a survey conducted on individuals who volunteered in the past year, an impressive 76% reported feeling physically better, a whopping 94% said that volunteering improved their mood, and 78% experienced reduced stress levels. So, by lending a hand to others, you not only make a difference but also enhance your own well-being and hopefulness.

Here are 8 ways that you can cultivate hope in the people around you:

Write Your Own Hope Journey

Now that you have the skills to create, maintain, and grow hope, your hope journey is up to you. Decide how you want to inspire hope in yourself and others, and then use your positive feelings and inspired actions to make it a reality.

Teach Hope

Remember, we are not born with hope; it is a skill we must be taught and many teens just like yourself are living life without these skills, so share this no-cost Hopeguide with your local schools, Boys and Girls Club, YMCA, place of worship, and more. To start exploring the Hopeful Minds curriculums today, visit www.hopefulminds.org/curriculums

Hang Posters for Hope

Put up posters and signs so that others can find the science of hope and start activating it in their own lives. Our resources are free for all here: www.hopefulcities.org/hang-posters-for-hope/

Create a Hope Initiative at your School

How can your school more successfully help students move from hopelessness to hope? Student-run initiatives like starting a Hope Club or implementing the iFred Five Day Global Hope Challenge are great ways to influence positive changes on campus.
www.globalhopechallenge.com

Put up Yard Signs for Hope

Yard Signs can be placed in your yard or your window to share the message of hope with your community. The purpose of the sign is to spread the message of the power of hope and encourage people to start learning about hope and using hope tools. All of our yard signs are both free for download and available for purchase at CafePress:
www.hopefulcities.org/put-up-yard-signs-for-hope/

Plant a Sunflower Garden for Hope

We use the sunflower as the global symbol for hope. The sunflower is based on the rebranding work by iFred, focusing on universal symbolism to create a "brand" for hope. The power of a brand is strong. We encourage you to plant a garden in your yard, in a pot on your windowsill (there are small sunflower species), or start a school community garden of sunflowers. Hope is always better when shared. Find out more here:
www.hopefulcities.org/plant-a-sunflower-garden-for-hope/

Get Support

Everyone needs help sometimes, and it is so important to be proactive about your hope: **www.hopefulcities.org/get-support**

Become a Hope Ambassador

A Hope Ambassador volunteers to be the person anyone in the school can go to when they need support or resources. Showcase that you are an ambassador using a Hope Ambassador pin or sticker found on our store at **www.theshinehopestore.com**

Make a Plan to Spread Hope

Discuss and make a plan for how your group can teach others about hope.

Who will your group reach out to about hope skills?

When will your group reach out to the individual(s)/organization?

What will your group say to them to convince them that hope is important?

How will your group facilitate teaching hope to them?

Create a Hope Cheat Sheet

Life is busy, and it is very easy to forget to practice new skills. Using the space below, draw, write, or use printed-out images to create a hope cheat sheet that includes the following information:

Your top 3 Stress Skills

1. _____   3. _____

2. _____

Your top 3 Happiness Habits

1. _____   3. _____

2. _____

Your top 2 Inspired Actions for school

1. _____

2. _____

One person who is in your Nourishing Network that will hold you accountable and support you in practicing hope skills.

Three strategies for Eliminating Challenges.

MALALA YOUSAFZAI

When Malala Yousafzai was just 15 years old, she was shot in the head on her way home from school in Pakistan. Malala was targeted by the Taliban for being outspoken about the importance of education for women.

However, the attack did not silence Malala. Instead, it gave her a global platform from which to speak. Malala continued to fight for women's educational rights. At age 17, she was awarded the Nobel Peace Prize for her dedication to giving all girls access to education.

Since that time, Malala has continued to give women around the world the support and resources they need to succeed. After graduating from college in 2020, Malala partnered with Literati on a book club called Fearless, in which she shared books by female first-time authors.

When asked about her choice, Malala said, "I want to focus on women who are writing their first books because there's a lot of fear and they're scared about how their book would be received, so it is important that we support those first-time writers, that we support young, feminist writers."

Malala understands the importance of providing people, especially young women, with resources and support to help them succeed. The hope resources in your workbook are there to help you continue to succeed on your hope journey.*

This story was created from publicly available information. It does not suggest endorsement of Hopeful Minds, or any affiliation by known celebrity to our program. All information is for illustrative purposes for youth, to demonstrate skills used to create, maintain, and grow hope.

☀ MY SHINE HOPE STORY™

Check out here to get your hope score.

To write your own shine hope story, spend 20% of your time writing about your challenge, and 80% of the time sharing strategies for how you overcame it so others can learn from you. Here's how:

☀ _____ 1. Write your name in the yellow line next to the box (feel free to use a nickname or anything else).

2. Put your favorite photo on the yellow box, or an image of something that represents you.

3. Write an introduction to your story explaining the challenge you faced. Explain the two ingredients of hopelessness: despair (feelings) and helplessness (inability to act) you experienced.

 4. Share sadness, anger, fear, or other feelings, and choose **3 Stress Skills** you used to naviate them (from the Shine infographic, or choose your own!).

5. Share **3 Happiness Habits** you used to get back to your upstairs brain.

 6. Talk about **3 Inspired Actions** you took, or share how you chunked down goals, the types of goals you set, or if you had to regoal.

7. Share who was in your **Nourishing Network**, and how they helped you navigate the challenge.

8. Pick 3 challenges from the **'Eliminating Challenges'** on the infographic, and share how you eliminated them.

 9. Write your conclusion. What do you want the world to know? What do you wish someone had told you? What is the moral of the story?

If you're inspired, share your story so we can help activate these skills globally.

#Hope #ShineHope #MyShineHopeStory

We all experience moments of hopelessness (emotional despair and motivational helplessness). The key is to use the Shine Hope skills to navigate your way from despair to positive feelings, and helplessness to inspired actions. Use the Shine Hope framework to build your muscle.

☀ Kathryn Goetzke

When I was 18 years old, a freshman at the University of Iowa, I called home and heard an unfamiliar, deep voice on the other line. It wasn't anyone I recognized, and he asked for my mom. My mom got on the phone to tell me my dad had taken his life. In that instance, my whole world crumbled. I felt a sadness so deep I thought I would never survive, and a helplessness so profound as I could not bring him back.

As hard as it was, I had to move forward. I started using Stress Skills to manage my pain. I cried when I was sad, started boxing to manage my anger, and learned how to start belly breathing to manage my fear. I listened to a lot of calming music when things got hard, and I started hiking all over the world. I also learned how to use sensory engagement to bring myself to the present moment.

Happiness Habits were critical. Sleep became an important part of my routine, and I started eating healthier foods. I cut alcohol out of my life. I replaced smoking with running, and made comedy clubs and laughter a part of my life. I listened to music, turned my sensory engagement passion into a purpose and started a company, and made volunteering a regular part of my life. I used dancing and live concerts (like my fave The Killers) as a form of release.

I also was very intentional about Inspired Actions. I had to chunk down my goals, leaving school and taking only one year at a time until I graduated. I had to regoal from having experiences with my dad to finding father-like figures to be in my life. I got closer to my brothers, their kids, and found mentors like Paul Carter and Dr. Belfer to guide me on my journey. My mom is my rock, my greatest source of strength and inspiration, keeping me moving forward towards my dreams.

Nourishing Networks were a constant. I stayed close to my friends and family, traveling, dancing, studying, and laughing. They were so compassionate, kind, generous, fun, and helped me heal. I forgave my dad for leaving, and forgave myself for not being there for him when he needed me. I got very close to God, understanding that I couldn't save my dad, and that in time this lesson would teach me how to help others.

It wasn't easy to Eliminate Challenges like rumination, internalizing failure, or worry. Yet I studied sensory engagement to be present when my mind started running. I deconstructed what led to my dad taking his life in a way that made it clear how to save myself and others. I knew that I couldn't control my dad, just like I can't control others. So I have focused on creating programming yet not being attached to if people want to learn it.

It's not been the easiest journey, and takes work. Yet by using the Shine Hope framework I have created a new life that is full of wonder, awe, happiness, adventure, and meaning. A different one than I expected, yet a beautiful one because I was able to dive in my pain, and learn the lessons necessary to teach others. And I use all my dad taught me in business to create a Shine Hope model for the world that ensures all know the what, why, and how of hope. And for that I know he is so very proud.

No matter what life brings, Keep Shining.

#Hope #ShineHope #MyHopeStory

MY SHINE HOPE STORY™

To add image in this area, edit the PDF via Adobe Acrobat or any PDF app editor.

#Hope #ShineHope #MyHopeStory

© 2024 The Shine Hope Company LLC.

the
shine hope
company

198

MY HOPE HERO

HOW HOPEFUL ARE YOU?

Did you measure your hope? The lower your score, the more you want to practice these skills! Remember, hope is a muscle we need to build it (add it).

Check out here to get your hope score.

To write your hope hero journey, spend 20% of your time writing about their challenge, and 80% of the time sharing strategies for how they overcame it so others can learn from it. Here's how:

 1. Write your hope hero's name in the yellow line next to the box (feel free to use a nickname or anything else).

 2. Put your favorite photo of them on the yellow box, or an image of something that represents your hope hero.

 3. Write an introduction explaining the challenge they faced. Explain the two ingredients of hopelessness: despair (feelings) and helplessness (inability to act) they experienced.

 4. Share sadness, anger, fear, or other feelings, and choose 3 **Stress Skills** they used to navigate them (from the Shine infographic, or choose your own!).

 5. Share 3 **Happiness Habits** they used to get back to upstairs brain.

 6. Talk about 3 **Inspired Actions** they took, or share how your hope hero chunked down goals, the types of goals they've set, or if they had to regoal.

 7. Share who was in their **Nourishing Network**, and how it helped them navigate the challenge.

 8. Pick 3 challenges from the '**Eliminating Challenges**' on the infographic, and share how your hope hero eliminated them.

 9. Write the conclusion. What do you want the world to know? What do you wish someone had told you? What is the moral of the story?

If you're inspired, share this hope hero story so we can help activate these skills globally!

#Hope #ShineHope #MyHopeHero

> We all experience moments of hopelessness (emotional despair and motivational helplessness). The key is to use the Shine Hope skills to navigate your way from despair to positive feelings, and helplessness to inspired actions. Use the Shine Hope framework to build your muscle.

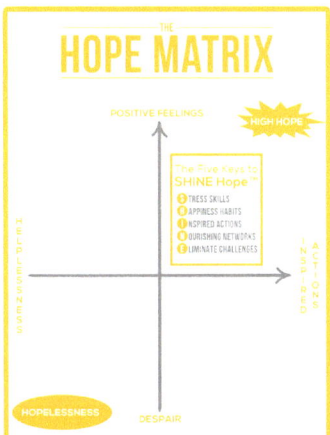

MY HOPE HERO

 Kathryn Goetzke

When Kathryn was 18 years old, a freshman at the University of Iowa, her dad died by suicide. It really changed her life. When she was in her early 20's, she then tried to take her own life, yet didn't tell another soul for 10 years. She knows a lot about hopelessness.

 To work on her recovery, she used a lot of Stress Skills. She talks about crying, going to therapy, learning to meditate, deep breathing, and listening to music. She traveled a lot, and took up hiking and exercise. She also took up boxing and spent a lot of time in nature.

 Kathryn was diligent about her Happiness Habits. She listened to her favorite band the Killers, went to concerts, focused on her nutrition and sleep, and started exercising. She pursued her passions, started a nonprofit iFred, and did a lot of volunteer work. She got serious about her purpose.

 Kathryn also took a lot of Inspired Actions towards her goals. She chunked them down, got a degree and then an MBA. She couldn't talk to her dad anymore, so she found business mentors. Her brothers were always there to support her, and her mom was a source of strength and inspiration.

 Kathryn spent a lot of time with her Nourishing Networks. She spent time with people that were kind, compassionate, fun, and helped her heal. She had a therapist and got close to God. She had animals and spent a lot of time with wild horses in Nevada.

 She worked to Eliminate Challenges like her rumination and worry. She learned about sensory engagement, and even started a company to teach others. She worked to forgive herself and others. She focused on what she could control, which was her present and future, and did her best to let go of the rest. She put all her failures into teaching others.

Her use of the Shine Hope framework led her on a much healthier path. She has been sober almost 20 years, and had her nonprofit that same amount of time. She is a representative at the United Nations for the World Federation for Mental Health, and has shared her story around the world at places like the World Bank, Harvard, the United Nations, and more. She has created programming to teach hope to kids, published papers, and is now doing workplace programming, has a college, course, and is activating cities. She is on a mission to ensure all know how to hope, one person at a time. She is an inspiration, and someone that truly lives by example practicing all she teaches.

#Hope #ShineHope #MyHopeHero

MY HOPE HERO

#Hope #ShineHope #MyHopeStory

the
shine hope
company

LESSON TAKEAWAY (GROUP DISCUSSION):

☀ *How might activating your communities impact your own hope?*

☀ *What is one piece of information you found most helpful in this lesson?*

☀ *How will you incorporate the information you learned in this lesson to your life this week?*

☀ *How did Malala use her passion and global platform to activate hope on a community scale?*

WEEKLY HOPE ACTIVATION

Inspired Actions for Hope are the things you can do to reinforce these lessons and begin to bring hope skills into your daily life. Choose at least one of the actions below to complete before moving to the next lesson.

☀ Set a SMART goal for the next steps in your hope journey.

☀ Teach a friend about hope and give them a copy of this Hopeguide.

☀ Plant a sunflower garden and put in a garden for hope sign *(Page 196)*

☀ Share your experiences about learning hope with others

☀ Complete an exit survey here to let us know your thoughts about the Hopeguide, what you liked, and what you would improve, so we can continue making this a program you want to use! *(Scan QR for Exit Survey at Page 196)*

☀ Paint a hope mural.

NOTES

Post your completed activities on social media using the following hashtags to help us teach the lessons. Make sure to tag us @ifredorg and @theshinehopecompany.

#HopefulMindsTeens #Hope #ShineHope #ScienceofHope #ActivatingHope
#MyHopeStory #HopefulCities #InternationalDayofHope #HopefulMinds

MY HOPE JOURNAL

1. How are you using your hope tools to succeed? Think about the SHINE acronym and how you've used it.

2. How has hope helped you overcome obstacles?

3. What SMART goals do you have for the future?

4. What can you control about the school year? What can't you control? How can you make the most of what they can control? How can you release emotions from what they can't control? How can you be creative about their experience this semester or year?

5. How do you define a hero? What do you think are some of the qualities in a hero? How does this person use hope tools in their life?

Please tag us on social media @ifredorg @theshinehopecompany to share your completed work and use the hashtags: #HopefulMinds #Hope #ShineHope #FiveKeysToShineHope #GrowHope #WhatAndWhyOfHope

MY HOPE JOURNAL

MY HOPE JOURNAL

MY HOPE JOURNAL

RESOURCES

Hope Research
Database

Paint A Sunflower
Mural for Hope

Adult Hope Scale
(Ages 16+)

Children's Hope
Scale (Ages 8-16)

Strengths Finder

Plant a Sunflower
Garden

Hopeful Cities

Hormones During
Teen Years

Goal Meditation
Music

Mindfulness
Exercise #1

Mindfulness
Exercise # 2

Exit Survey

Where to Find
Support

ADDITIONAL RESOURCES

Hopeful Minds is based on the research that hope is teachable. The aim is to equip all students, teachers, and parents with the tools they need to define, learn, and grow a Hopeful Mind. The Hopeful Minds curriculums and resources are available for download at www.hopefulminds.org/curriculums

The Five-Day Global Hope Challenge is a daily challenge that introduces the Five Keys to Shine Hope that everyone can use to activate hope within their lives and their community. The challenge is ideal for governments, workplaces, schools, and more. Sign-up today at www.hopefulcities.org

Friendship Bench's mission is to get people out of kufungisisa - depression & anxiety - by creating safe spaces and a sense of belonging in communities to improve mental wellbeing and enhance quality of life. To learn more and request a bench placed in your area, visit www.friendshipbenchzimbabwe.org

Karma Box Project is a community initiative allowing people to give non-perishable food, hygiene products, toiletries, and other useful items to those in need. The boxes are filled up with the goods by anyone in the community and someone in need can take items from the box as needed. To learn more, visit www.karmaboxproject.org

One World Strong Foundation created the ResilienceNet Mobile App, which empowers and provides support to local, regional, and national terrorism prevention practitioners, relevant frontline responders and individual Americans seeking support. To learn more about the One World Strong Foundation and download their app, visit www.oneworldstrong.org/copy-of-how-we-do-it

National Alliance on Mental Illness (NAMI) is America's largest grassroots mental health organization dedicated to building better lives for Americans affected by mental illness. NAMI offers an abundance of resources for those navigating mental illness or for those seeking to learn more.
Find more at www.nami.org/home

Choose Love Movement nurtures safer and more loving communities through next generation essential life skills and character development programs for all stages of life. Choose Love is an evidence-based curriculum that will help students feel safer, learn better, and achieve more! Find out more at www.chooselovemovement.org

Hope Means Nevada works to eliminate teen suicide and empower Nevada's youth to live hopeful lives. Find out more at www.hopemeansnevada.org

One Mind catalyzes visionary change through science, business and media to transform the world's mental health. Find out more at www.onemind.org

Charter for Compassion supports the emerging global movement that brings compassion to life. It is a global network connecting people, cities, grassroots organizers and leaders to each other. It provides educational resources, organizing tools, and avenues for communication. Find out more at www.charterforcompassion.org

Hopeful Mindsets®

Hopeful Mindsets® is a framework that uses the Five Keys to Shine Hope to apply to any challenge in life. It is based on the work of leading experts on Hope, Mindset, Mental Health, Stress, Positive Psychology, Business, Communications, and more. Using the Five Keys to Shine Hope as a foundation, Hopeful Mindsets introduces critical hope skills to help anyone move from hopelessness to hope.

The initial program, Hopeful Mindsets on the College Campus, is a 10-module video course from The Shine Hope Company that equips students with crucial hope skills through expert insights and real-life stories. The course features experts from Harvard, Stanford, and Columbia, with insights from recent college graduates that offer real-life practical strategies and stories from their experiences with homelessness, mental health diagnoses, death, violence, and everyday challenges at school.

The Hopeful Mindsets General Overview is a 90-minute video course for anyone that introduces hope and the Five Keys to Shine Hope framework to help you create, maintain, and grow hope in your life. This course is taught by Kathryn Goetzke, based on her knowledge of mental health and hope, and her work to date. It compiles knowledge from leading experts on Hope, Mindset, Mental Health, Stress, Positive Psychology, Business, Communications, and includes video lessons, a full downloadable workbook and exercises to practice skills for hope, and is available individually or to license for organizations.

The Hopeful Mindsets Workplace Overview is a 90-minute video course for the workplace that introduces hope and the Five Keys to Shine Hope™ framework to help you create, maintain, and grow hope in the workplace. We give an overview of the framework, so you can then apply it to your career to activate hope at work. The course is available for individuals or to license to entire companies, to ensure all know the what, why, and how of hope.

You can learn more about the Hopeful Mindsets courses at www.hopecourses.com.

Hopeful Cities®

Hopeful Cities© is equipping cities around the world with the tools they need to create, maintain, and grow hope, citywide. Learn how you can activate hope in your community at www.hopefulcities.org.

Hopeful Minds

Hopeful Minds® is programming for youth based on research that suggests hope is teachable (a skill). The aim is to equip students, teachers, and parents with the tools they need to define, learn, and grow Hopeful Minds in young kids. Learn more at www.hopefulminds.org.

the
shine hope
company

The Shine Hope Company™ - Our mission is to improve lives globally by teaching scientifically informed and evidence-based methods to measure and cultivate hope. Learn how to activate hope in your life and community at www.theshinehopecompany.com.